ABOVE EVERY OTHER DESIRE:

A CENTENNIAL HISTORY OF JOHNSON BIBLE COLLEGE

1893-1993

ABOVE EVERY OTHER DESIRE:

A CENTENNIAL HISTORY OF JOHNSON BIBLE COLLEGE

1893-1993

by

L. Thomas Smith, Jr.

November 4, 1992

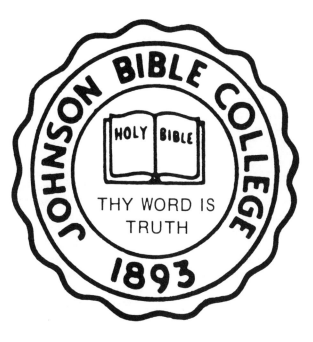

JOHNSON BIBLE COLLEGE

HOLY BIBLE

THY WORD IS
TRUTH

1893

Faith
Prayer
Work

A CENTENNIAL TRIBUTE
TO
JOHNSON BIBLE COLLEGE

One hundred years of service
    for the Lord, it all began . . .
When God gave a special mission
    to a very special man
The Christian Church/Churches of Christ
    had not until this day,
A Bible college to prepare
    young men to preach "The Way."
On Founder's Day, the twelfth of May,
    eighteen hundred and ninety-three,
The cornerstone was first laid
    showing it to be
The School of the Evangelists,
    born of faith and work and prayer
That poor boys with desire to preach
    might live and study there.
From seed that Ashley Johnson planted
    seven years before,
His Correspondence Bible Course
    was opening the door.

Dr. Ashley and Emma Johnson
    gave their treasure, talent, time
To the school that was to bear his name
    in nineteen hundred and nine.
Through trials, famine, floods and fire
    they never knew despair,
The clouds of doubt were blotted out
    by faith and work and prayer.
On December one, nineteen hundred four
    Old Main burned to the ground.
When he returned home Sunday noon
    a sad Ashley Johnson found
Seventy-five of his boys had lined
    his walk in sympathy
And sang, through tears, his favorite hymn,
    "My Faith Looks Up To Thee."
For a hundred years they've served to be
    her strength and guiding light,
The Upper Room for private prayer,
    the prayer service every night.

Endowments, grants, and wealthy friends
    the college did not know,
But from appeals by voice and pen
    the school began to grow.
The new Old Main soon graced the Hill
    next to Old Dusty, as she was known,
The Emma Johnson Industrial Hall,
    the working students' home.
They manned the farm, the cannery,
    they milked the dairy herd,
At night by lamps of kerosene
    they studied from "The Word."
In seventy-five, the school was blessed
    by the generous gift that came
Of the new multipurpose building
    that bears the donors' names.
Men and women students, teachers,
    striving daily to prepare,
Laborers for the fields of harvest
    led by faith and work and prayer.

Affectionately referred to as
    the White House residence,
This stately eighteen ninety home
    has served all her presidents.
In nineteen hundred and twenty-five
    God called Ashley Johnson home,
Until her death in twenty-seven
    Mrs. Johnson served on alone.
Dr. Alva Ross Brown was Johnson's choice
    for the work he had begun,
With Alma, Bob and Betty, he led
    until his death in forty-one.
Dr. Bell, his wife Myrtle and Betty,
    like Brown, a Johnson graduate,
Led the school with deep commitment
    until his death in sixty-eight.
At home with God, whose message
    they each lived to proclaim,
Their earthly forms lie resting
    in the shadow of Old Main.

In sixty-nine, Dr. David Eubanks
  became the school's fifth president,
With wife, Margaret, at his side
  his true help-mate in every sense,
Sons, David, Jr., Philip, daughter, Linnie,
  all five Johnson graduates
Where Dr. Eubanks started teaching
  in nineteen hundred fifty-eight.
With the college Council of Seventy
  and board of JBC Trustees
A dedicated college staff,
  and a committed faculty,
The college stands on solid rock
  through those the Lord has led,
And looks to God's tomorrow
  for His victories ahead.
An old remembered slogan
  guides the school year after year,
"A Preacher-Training Institution
  in a Preacher-Growing Atmosphere."

Three hundred and fifty acres
  of fond memories, precious sights,
In the foothills of the Smokies . . .
  Johnson's beloved Kimberlin Heights.
With the French Broad River flowing
  by the White House on the north,
Where once the steamer, Annabelle King,
  proudly traveled back and forth.
The lotus pond, Johnson Island
  the students used to till,
The mule wagon coal train
  from Burnett's station to the Hill.
The celebrated Kissing Oak
  with its fond memory,
Where for thirty years the Johnsons kissed
  each time they passed beneath the tree.
Then, there's the Poland-China hogs
  about which Johnson one time said,
"They're going to enter the ministry"
  that the preachers might be fed.

What faith, prayer and work can do
  is here for all to see,
At Johnson Bible College
  east of Knoxville, Tennessee.
The dairy barn is gone
  that graced the scene of yesterdays,
Dormitories stand where once
  the Holsteins used to graze.
New buildings reaching upwards
  through skeletons of steel,
As friends respond supporting
  Dr. Eubanks' pledge appeal.
From a forty-two enrollment
  in the first year of her birth,
Thousands now have passed her doors
  to preach "The Word" throughout the earth.
One hundred years of service
  for the Lord, it all began . . .
When God gave a special mission
  to a very special man.

Charles W. Swisher
Honorary Alumnus
Crown Point, Indiana
Copyright, 1989

CONTENTS

PREFACE

When I told my respected adviser and friend at the University of Tennessee that I was going to write a centennial history of Johnson Bible College, he gave me two warnings: "Don't do it," and "If you are going to do it, don't make it a history of the presidents of the college." I have unapologetically disregarded both pieces of advice. Having written my master's thesis on Ashley Johnson and the School of the Evangelists, I had intended to continue my research on the history of the college and was overjoyed to accept Dr. Eubanks's request to write a history for the centennial celebration. I realize the inherent dangers and am quite familiar with the French *philosophe* Voltaire's maxim that those who dare to write contemporary history will be reprimanded for both what they include and what they leave out!

I have also chosen to organize the history around the terms of the presidents of the college. One might criticize this study as simply a biography of the presidents rather than a history of the school, or that it views events "from the top down" while overlooking less prominent but no less valuable contributions from others. I chose to organize the material in this way because of the unique roles that the presidents have played in establishing and maintaining the mission and character of the college. It is also interesting that the presidential terms closely parallel the major periods in late-nineteenth and twentieth century American history, which enabled me to more clearly construct the historical backgrounds for each chapter. Although organization of the material reflects the presidential terms, all aspects of the life of the institution—administration, faculty, students, alumni, facilities, and curriculum—have been considered and included.

Two principles have guided my research and writing: readability and brevity. I wanted to provide an overview of the history of the college in order to communicate the "essence" of its character. I have avoided lengthy anecdotes, statistics, and lists. I have attempted to write in a straight-forward narrative style, avoiding both a self-serving "public relations" approach and a critical history written solely for academics. It is by no means an exhaustive history: many important events and developments, as well as numerous people who have made extremely significant contributions to the college, have been omitted. I acknowledge the perspective on the history of the college offered by Dr. Floyd E. Clark as he concluded his 1992 Founder's Day message: "It will take an eternity to tell all the stories."

I have used a variety of primary sources including college catalogs, official publications such as the *Blue and White,* self-study reports, annual presidential reports, academic and financial statistics, archival letters and notes, published and unpublished works of its presidents and faculty, audio cassettes, journals such as the *Christian Standard,* student annuals, and oral interviews. Secondary sources include theses, biographies, and earlier histories of the college (in print, audio, and video). I have tried to keep footnotes at a minimum. When the source is obvious from the text, or when the material was derived from a variety of sources (i.e., compilations such as enrollment and financial statistics), I have not included the reference.

I deeply appreciate the cooperation and contribution of Helen Lemmon, Wilbur Reid, Jr., Joel Rood and their staffs. I would like to thank my research assistant, Terry Duncan, for her untiring labor. President David Eubanks' invaluable contributions to the manuscript and words of encouragement have been received with gratitude. No one completes a project such as this without the generous support of family and colleagues. I have received this support in far greater measure than I deserve.

Finally, this history is designed for the general reader, regardless of his or her familiarity with the college. I certainly assume, however, that the vast majority of readers will be alumni and friends of the college. It is my intent that the reader of this history will understand the character of the institution and the significant events that have shaped its development, so that he or she might more fully appreciate the heritage of Johnson Bible College. It is my prayer that I have faithfully discharged my duties.

PROLOGUE

Some things have not changed in one hundred years at the college on Kimberlin Heights. The French Broad River still ambles slowly along the campus' northern border around Johnson Island and toward the nearby fork where it joins the Holston River. The dense fog envelops the approximately three hundred and fifty acres on cool autumn mornings. The "Prayer Oak" stands its silent vigil in the clearing near the presidential cemetery. A herd of cattle (though now diminished in quantity and quality) wanders through one of the several pastures that remain. "Johnson Boys"—the students who have come to this place to live and study—rise early in the morning and rush off to class or work. The vision that brought this college into being, the desire to teach the Bible to the young man "who desires above every other desire" to preach the gospel of Jesus Christ, still lives in its trustees, administration, and faculty. In one sense, the person who walked on "the Hill" in 1893 would find familiar surroundings today.

In another sense, however, so much has changed that our visitor from one hundred years ago might think he or she is completely lost. In addition to the influx of twentieth century technology (and Johnson Bible College boasts the latest in computers and communications), the complex of classroom, administration, library, dormitory, recreation, and worship facilities surprises even the visitor from a quarter-century ago. There are as many "Johnson Girls" as boys among the student body. Educational programs and methods, faculty qualifications, vocational opportunities, community involvement, church relations, financial support, student recruitment, administrative organization, and student life have changed considerably through the century of development.

This book is a story of change at Johnson Bible College. What has changed and what has stayed the same? Why has this changed or has not changed? How has the college adjusted to changes in society over which it has no control? In essence, the question that lies behind this study is, "How does this institution—Johnson Bible College—relate to its past?"

All institutions reflect in some way the initial concerns and personalities of those who brought them into being. In other words, they reflect their past. They are not self-perpetuating: they are dependent upon the dreams, labors, sacrifices, and objectives of the men and women who brought them into existence. There is a continuity with the past that gives the institution its unique character and contribution to human society.

From a historical perspective, there are three ways in which any institution relates to its past: (1) it can cling to the past, maintaining its original vision, goals, and methods with rigid orthodoxy; (2) it can ignore the past, leaving behind its original intent and character; or, (3) it can maintain a commitment to the concerns and principles of its founder(s) while, at the same time, readjusting its methods and widening its vision to meet the needs, demands, and problems of a changing context. An institution, especially one committed to learning, cannot obstinately cling to the past. If it refuses to re-orient itself to new challenges, it slowly dies. Very often an institution "corallizes": just as a coral reef (an immovable structure) is created by the skeletons of what were once living and thriving sea animals, so then the lifeless, rigid structures of an institution may remain long after the worthwhile efforts of its past are gone.

On the other hand, an institution usually falters when it leaves the path of its original intent. History is full of examples of men, women, and movements who distorted a noble cause into a contemptible enterprise. The institution that betrays or denies its "essence" has lost continuity with its past.

The third alternative—faithfulness to the original impetus yet flexibility in response to change—seems to suggest the "formula for success" of an institution. It cannot cling to the past nor lose sight of its origins. Therefore, it is essential that any institution recognize its original vision, motivation, and goals.

This recognition becomes the "rudder" by which the past guides the present. The institution honors its past by evaluating every response to changing contexts and challenges in the light of its original purpose.

This history of Johnson Bible College attempts to understand the dialogue between the college and its past. The monumental task of writing a centennial history is, in the author's view, lessened by this focus. Many stories about Johnson Bible College beg to be written: of presidents, students, faculty, work, ministries, and friends. The history of the college is full of dramatic events, both heroic and tragic. Although many of these stories are included, this book is not an anecdotal history of the college. Nor is it simply a chronology of names, dates, and events, although these are certainly important to any history. An institution such as Johnson Bible College is much more than a lifeless chronicle of when this person was born, this building was dedicated, or this course was inserted into the curriculum.

The purpose of this history is to identify and trace the development of the essential nature of Johnson Bible College, an educational institution founded for "the poor young man who desired above every other desire to preach the gospel." This "essence" may be reduced to three great concerns that were a part of the founder's original vision: for world evangelism, that the great commission might be fulfilled; for the poor and disadvantaged, that they might have equal opportunity to share in the task of evangelism; for Bible-centered education, that the evangelist might be fully equipped for his or her task. The college has faced significant challenges that threaten its existence and its historic purpose. It has been forced to change to meet a new context. The motivation for this study is to seek understanding of how Johnson Bible College has remained faithful to its purpose and how it has adapted to its world in its century of existence.

Chapter 1

A Kindled Desire
1857–1893

In late autumn, 1885, Ashley S. Johnson sat alone by the hearth of a small cabin in the pine woods of South Carolina contemplating the great need for workers to evangelize the impoverished region. He was serving his second term as the State Evangelist for the Disciples of Christ churches in South Carolina and had become sick while on a preaching tour. The other inhabitants of the cabin had retired for the evening and Johnson sat, "heavy with the weight of the world's woe." He felt great responsibility for the souls in his "field" and bemoaned the fact that the laborers were so few. He later recorded his deliberations of that dark, cold night:

> I was in the midst of the harvest alone, yet not alone, for God . . . was with me. I sat and thought, and unexpectedly it dawned upon me that I could teach men the gospel through the mails, and thus inspire them to proclaim it as they learned it.[1]

Ashley Johnson's "unexpected idea"—the Correspondence Bible College—was the spark that would kindle Johnson Bible College.

Most institutions have a very complex origin in which many factors, persons, and events play their respective parts. Johnson Bible College originated in the vision and persistent work of one man—Ashley S. Johnson. When this man proposed to transform his highly successful Correspondence Bible College (a home Bible study course by mail) into a bonafide educational institution, most of his friends and acquaintances were opposed to the idea. Even his wife, who had been an important co-laborer in the C.B.C., was skeptical. Therefore, the early history of the college, along with its basic goals, methods, and character, originated in the life and thought of Ashley Johnson.

Ashley Sidney Johnson was born on June 22, 1857, in Knox County, Tennessee, the eldest of the seven sons of Jeremiah and Barbara Johnson. Ashley's great-grandfather was Jacob Kimberlin, whose family owned the "Heights" above the French Broad River and for whom this community in south Knox County was named. Although Johnson's formal educational opportunities were limited, he was a bright student and an avid reader. His early education was supervised by his father at home after which he enrolled in two successive neighborhood "subscription schools." One of his teachers was Alexander S. Thompson, who took a special interest in his precocious pupil, providing additional studies and lending him books. Ashley Johnson took delight in relating his first meeting with Mr. Thompson:

> "What is your name?" he was asked.
> "Ashley Johnson, sir."
> "Can you read?"
> "Yes sir, I can read anything I ever saw."
> "Can you read Greek?"
> "I never saw any of that, sir."[2]

As a result of Thompson's tutelage, Johnson passed the county examination for a teacher's certificate at the age of seventeen. After a year's study at the University of Tennessee, Johnson entered the law office of J.C.J. Williams of Knoxville, with intentions of becoming a lawyer, while continuing to teach school on a limited basis.

His religious background was more limited. Johnson's father and mother were members of the Baptist church, but had "drifted into skepticism and . . . comparative indifference." Ashley described his lack of Christian training: "I was never in Sunday School . . . although my parents occasionally took me to church. I had a desire to be a Christian when I was only about twelve. I had no one to guide me, and in consequence became profane and godless."[3]

The Johnson family became acquainted with some Disciples preachers, notably Elder John Adcock, and the parents were soon persuaded to join the Disciples congregation which met near Thorn Grove. Ashley tried to remain indifferent to his family's religious awakening, but at the age of twenty experienced a thorough conversion after attending a Baptist revival meeting:

> In the midst of the great excitement which prevailed [at the revival], the thought came to me like a bolt from a clear sky at noonday: "Here I am, trifling my time away, knowing the truth, and these people are drifting to judgement in ignorance; I will turn over a new leaf and be a preacher." My mind was made up. I went home and told my parents. I began to study the New Testament under my father's help and when I was fully convinced as to what I ought to do, I wrote to a preacher to come and was immersed by Elder John Adcock on the 14th day of October, 1877.[4]

He later reflected on the intensity of his transformation: "If conversion is a complete turning, I was converted, for I turned my back on all my life-plans and ambitions and gave myself unreservedly to the work of Christ."[5] He began his work as an evangelist almost immediately: "On the following Saturday [after his immersion] I went to Thorn Grove to attend a meeting. The brethren knew my intentions and asked me to preach. I had never prayed in public."[6] Johnson was overjoyed with his new-found vocation and began an intense program of studying the Bible and reading the works of Alexander Campbell. His zeal for preaching was insatiable. He disclosed: "I used to get so full of the truth that I could only relieve my mind by preaching to the trees, which I often did. I preached also to people when I had the opportunity."[7] This evangelistic fervor was a hallmark of Johnson's life and became one of the essential components of Johnson Bible College.

Johnson soon embarked upon what would become a very successful career as an author. He began to publish a theological journal, the *Christian Watchman,* in 1879, and wrote his most popular book, *The Great Controversy,* in 1882. Johnson's works included a Bible encyclopedia (to be used as the primary reference book for his correspondence Bible lessons), a "self-interpreting" New Testament, Bible commentaries, hermeneutical and doctrinal studies, devotional literature, an autobiography, the record of a public debate, and collections of sermons. Much of the financial capital for the School of the

Evangelists was provided by the sale of these books. Johnson was an editorial correspondent of the *Christian Standard* from 1884 to 1886 and later contributed several articles. Two other journals, *Johnson's Quarterly* (1888-1892) and *The Querist* (1890), were edited by Johnson and were closely connected to his correspondence courses.

Johnson served as minister to the First Christian Church of Knoxville (for approximately six months) and to a small group who later organized the First Christian Church of Chattanooga (duration unknown). In the meantime, he gained notoriety among the churches as the author of *The Great Controversy* and was called to be the State Evangelist for South Carolina, employed jointly by the South Carolina Missionary Coopera- tion and the American Christian Missionary Society. Arriving on December 1, 1883, Johnson conducted a highly successful evangelistic campaign, reporting 124 additions in 118 days. It is not surprising that he later declared, "In that state I did my best work as a preacher."[8] Upon his return to Knoxville in late March, 1884, Johnson was employed by the Evangelizing Board of Tennessee to stir interest in cooperative missionary efforts among the churches in the eastern portion of the state. He traveled extensively throughout East Tennessee soliciting contributions for evangelistic and missionary work.

It is important to note that Ashley Johnson's missionary concern reflected one of the broader themes within American Christianity and churches of the Restoration Movement in the late-nineteenth century. One of the key developments within the American churches in this period was a resurgence of evan- gelical revivalism. Nearly every denomination had some type of evangelism or missionary program. The Presbyterians' "Committee on Aggressiveness" was typical of the various ef- forts. Major religious journals reported thousands of conver- sions weekly. Dwight L. Moody, the foremost of the urban evangelists, hit the American scene with fervor in 1873 and packed meeting halls in nearly all major cities. The decade from 1870 to 1880 saw the greatest percentage of growth in church membership in American history. In Tennessee, church membership grew from 22 percent of the population in 1875 to 32 percent in 1906. The last quarter of the nineteenth century in Tennessee saw a population growth of 72 percent while church affiliation increased 150 percent.[9]

This kind of numerical growth was also evident within the Restoration Movement. The Christian churches experienced their era of highest expansion from 1865 to 1900 with an increase in membership from 191,000 to 1.2 million persons. Throughout the country evangelistic efforts were rewarded with amazing results. In Tennessee alone church membership more than tripled from 1875 to 1906 (17,784 to 56,315). From the ashes of the ill-fated American Christian Missionary Society rose the Christian Women's Board of Missions (1874) and the Foreign Christian Missionary Society (1875) which supported highly successful mission enterprises in India, China, the Congo, and Japan. Various state cooperatives were started, including the Tennessee State Missionary Convention (1873), the North Carolina Christian Missionary Society (1870) and the South Carolina Missionary Cooperation (1883). Disciples entered the competition to evangelize the West. Aided by the Board of Church Extension, over eight hundred churches were erected in the West by 1904.[10]

A concern for education appeared as an important sidelight to this era of revival. The Sunday School movement gained increasing popularity under the leadership of B.F. Jacobs (one of Moody's associates) and the International Sunday School Association. The adoption of the Uniform Lesson Plan in 1872, the yearly conventions held in nearly every state, and the rise of teacher-training institutions inspired extensive organization of Sunday Schools and training of workers.

The Bible College movement was also an outgrowth of this evangelistic-educational concern. Since the colonial period evangelical Christianity had given leadership to higher education in America: Harvard, Yale, and Columbia Universities were initially minister-training institutions. The tremendous establishment and growth of colleges and universities in the early nineteenth century were often motivated by Protestant leadership. However, the development of tax-supported education, the expansion of Catholic higher education, and the increasing secularization of higher education drained the early biblical content and ministerial programs from such schools. S.A. Witmer has observed that the Bible College movement represented ". . . a restoration of Biblical authority and direction in education, and a return to the central concern of Christian education—the implementation of Christ's Great Commission."[11]

Seven Bible colleges (or institutes) were established in America in the late-nineteenth century: Nyack Missionary College (1883), Moody Bible Institute (1886), Western Baptist Bible College (1890), Johnson Bible College (School of the Evangelists, 1893), Northwest Christian College (Eugene Divinity School, 1895), Boston Bible College (1897), and Azusa Pacific College (1899). Toronto Bible College (now Ontario Bible College) was founded in Canada in 1894. While these schools sought different goals—Nyack was primarily interested in overseas missions, Moody with training lay persons for inter-city work, Johnson and Northwest with educating preachers for local congregations—they shared a common commitment to prepare students for Christian ministry through a program that centered around the Bible and practical training. They recognized the critical lack of trained personnel in the churches and missionary enterprises and the failure of the seminaries to prepare a sufficient number of persons for specialized ministries. These schools provided the impetus and the models for the more than 250 Bible colleges and institutes in existence today in the United States and Canada. Ashley Johnson's ministry and the original purpose of Johnson Bible College was molded in this era of intense revivalism.

After completing his work for the Evangelizing Association of Tennessee in the summer of 1884, Johnson attended the Philadelphia School of Elocution and Oratory in Grimsby Park, Ontario, Canada. It was here in Canada that he met and soon married Emma Elizabeth Strawn, his lifelong partner in his work and president of the college after his death. The couple enjoyed a brief ministry in New York and then moved back to South Carolina where Ashley began his second term as State Evangelist. His work among the impoverished people of upstate South Carolina brought further focus to his life's vocation: the need to educate those who desired to preach the Gospel but could not afford formal schooling.

Johnson had great empathy for the South and the "poor young boy." His work was concentrated primarily in the South (Tennessee, North Carolina, South Carolina, and Georgia) and he was quite familiar with the post-war social conditions of the region. Samuel Hill has noted the "unattractiveness" of Southern history following the war: bitterness, economic depression, and social dislocation. During the time of industrialization in the North and the great migrations to the West, the South was experiencing abject poverty in agriculture, drab life in the cotton mill villages, and explosive racial tension. The Civil War had brought physical devastation, governmental chaos, collapse of banking and transportational systems, and starvation to the southern people. East Tennessee experienced both scorn from the rest of the South and neglect by the authorities during Reconstruction because of its Unionist sentiment during the war. The problems associated with Reconstruction perpetuated these conditions in many areas far beyond the years assigned to this period in American history.[12]

A lack of educational opportunities is one example of the lingering problems of the South. Less than one-fifth of the population of Tennessee in 1872 had any means of education. In some counties there was not a single school—public or private—in operation. It was not until 1909 that one-fourth of Tennessee's tax revenue was allotted to education. The situation was worse in South Carolina.[13]

Ashley Johnson demonstrated a keen sense of solidarity with the people of the South: "I was born and born again in the midst of the vast field of the South, the fairest land under the sun to myriads."[14] Having been raised in relative poverty, Johnson sympathized with people who lived in poverty and resented those who were not sensitive to the plight of the poor. Johnson wrote to the *Christian Standard* in 1883:

> I am sorry to say that in many of our churches the poor, the off-cast, downtrodden are not seen. The great rush in my localities seems to be for the rich, the great, the influential. The churches . . . are becoming social clubs. The poor man is not at home. He feels that he is not wanted. He seeks for associations elsewhere and loses his interest in religion.[15]

Confronted with poverty in the communities and churches, Johnson sought the answer in educating poor boys to preach and sending them back into their home areas. Johnson's plea in the *Christian Standard* in 1907 clearly summarized his concern:

I am sending out one thousand personal letters to the preachers of the South, urging them to put us in touch with the Southern boys who wish to preach. Our doors are open to such boys from anywhere, from everywhere, but the need in the South is so great, so widespread, so insatiable, that I am making this special effort. Poverty does not bar a young man from the School of the Evangelists.[16]

As Ashley Johnson sat by the fire in the remote cabin in South Carolina, two overwhelming concerns were on his mind: the preaching of the gospel and the education of the poor young man. He soon announced his scheme that was conceived on that night, writing in the January 1886 issue of the *Christian Standard*:

I have a plan by which I can assist young men who are laboring to qualify themselves to preach the Gospel. Thorough course of instruction at a very small cost, and no necessity of leaving home. Five months trial, and if not satisfactory, no cost whatever. I think the plan will furnish assistance for at least one hundred students. All letters answered immediately.[17]

Four years later over a thousand had been enrolled, with two to three hundred pupils actively studying with Dr. Johnson each year. He announced an enrollment of three hundred in the January 2, 1892 *Christian Standard*. The *Knoxville Daily Tribune* reported in June 1891 that Johnson had 225 to 230 students "in all parts of the country, every State and Territory being represented."

Johnson called the Correspondence Bible College "the most thorough and comprehensive course of Bible Study on earth."[18] It consisted of twenty-eight lessons with over three thousand questions to be completed in a four year span. Each "manuscript" must have been completed by the student and examined by Johnson before work could be started on the succeeding one. It was a tedious—but certainly thorough—method of Bible study. Dr. Johnson wrote the *Condensed Biblical Cyclopedia* (later called the *Busy Man's Bible Encyclopedia*) as a companion volume to the C.B.C. lessons. *Johnson's Quarterly* furnished a line of communication to the students, along with study aids, devotional thoughts, exhortation, and advertisements of the "college" and Johnson's books. The *Quarterly* also printed students' essays, poetry, and sermon outlines.

The C.B.C. claimed a total enrollment of nearly three thousand students from 1886 to 1912. Among its many graduates were S.S. Lappin (preacher, educator, and editor of *Christian Standard*), Hall L. Calhoun (professor at the College of the Bible), H.L. Veach (professor at Drake University), Mattee W. Burgess (missionary to India), A.J. Thompson (president of Louisville Bible School), and C.E. Underwood (president of Eureka College). The C.B.C. became a secondary concern to Johnson after the establishment of the School of the Evangelists, but continued to have a limited function.

In honor of his work as an evangelist and an educator Johnson was awarded two honorary degrees: Master of Arts from Hiram College (Ohio) in 1889 and Doctor of Laws (Ll.D) from Christian University (now Culver-Stockton College), Canton, Missouri, in 1891 (he was later awarded an honorary Masters degree from Johnson Bible College). The June 5, 1891 edition of the *Knoxville Daily Tribune* announced his honorary doctorate from Christian University with this note: "Professor Johnson's many friends in this city and in all parts of the South congratulate him on receiving such a high honor from an institution which ranks so high among educational institutions in the United States." By 1892, thirty-five year old Ashley Johnson was recognized by his community and church as an evangelist, author, and innovative educational leader.

The practical advice that Johnson gave to his students in the *Quarterly* revealed a man with depth of insight concerning the Bible and preaching. His commitment to education and thorough preparation of preachers of the gospel was expressed in an essay entitled, "Do Not Be in a Hurry to Preach":

> One of the chief difficulties in teaching young men who desire to preach is that many of them are not willing to wait, and therefore begin to preach before they are fully qualified to do so. This is simply mistaken zeal. Every man who expects to preach should . . . under no circumstances allow the public to consider him a preacher until he is well qualified to be one. . . . It is a fact that a man cannot preach successfully without a thorough knowledge of the Scriptures. We encourage young men to enter the ministry. We encourage them also to qualify themselves before entering actively into the work.[19]

Considering the fact that Johnson was pressed into preaching one week after his baptism, this bit of preaching wisdom was probably gained through painful experience! Johnson's list of "Don'ts" for young preachers contained several "pearls" of wisdom:

> Don't preach without preparation; it indicates that you are wanting in appreciation of the responsibility that rests upon you.
>
> Don't assume in the pulpit or anywhere else that you are Sir Oracle; better informed men than yourself will be disgusted with you and your pretensions.
>
> Don't fish for compliments by belittling your work; let praise come spontaneously.
>
> Don't put yourself forward for greater positions; fill your humble station well and greater places will seek you.
>
> Don't try to drive people to heaven; sheep will follow if the shepherd will call them kindly.
>
> Don't use big words for show; make the weakest understand you.
>
> Don't be discourteous to those who disagree with you; others are perhaps as sincere as you are.
>
> Don't preach too long; the true worth of a sermon is as often in its brevity as in its length.
>
> Don't preach from manuscript; imagine Paul on Mars Hill, preaching to the cultured men of Greece with one eye on a pile of manuscript and the other on the people!
>
> Don't expect the people to do any more of what you preach than what you do yourself; be an example as well as a preacher.
>
> Don't be in a hurry to marry; hundreds of young men have been ruined by thoughtless and premature marriages.
>
> Don't enter into controversy with every person who doubts your conclusions; a still tongue is proof of a wise head.
>
> Don't be haughty; be a man of the people.
>
> Some old preachers might read this with profit![20]

The Johnsons moved from South Carolina to Augusta, Georgia, in the winter of 1885 where Ashley preached and conducted the C.B.C. for one year. They returned to Knoxville in 1886 and operated the correspondence school full-time. Reflecting on this experience, Johnson wrote:

> Finally our correspondence became so great that I was forced to practically give up preaching and give myself to teaching. Money flowed to us continually. Just here we made the mistake of

our lives. We thought the money belonged to us, and used it accordingly. We built a nice residence in Knoxville, and were enjoying our selfish lives immensely, when I had another inspiration.[21]

This new project was a "more permanent school" to educate preachers. Two circumstances contributed to this concern: Johnson's recognition that many of the "poor boys" lacked an adequate English education to complete the correspondence courses and the presence of Albert T. Fitts in the Johnson home. Johnson had baptized Fitts and his father in an evangelistic meeting in South Carolina and was impressed with the boy's academic potential. Fitts joined the Johnsons in Knoxville, lived in their home, and studied under Dr. Johnson for two years prior to the founding of the School of the Evangelists. Johnson envisioned a college where more young men like Fitts could prepare for the ministry.

Such a venture, however, seemed beyond Johnson's means. He confessed:

> The School of the Evangelists was burning on the altar of my heart. I told my wife about it. She could not comprehend it. I wrote to my friends about it. They gave me the greatest discouragement of which they were capable! I was alone so far as "like flesh and blood" was concerned.[22]

After fruitlessly seeking a location in Knoxville to establish a school, he purchased his old homestead—the 175 acre Jacob Kimberlin farm about twelve miles outside of Knoxville—and proceeded to move to the country. Johnson constructed his house (completed in 1890 and now called the White House) and persuaded another young man, John B. Dickson (a correspondence student from South Carolina), to join him. In spite of discouragement from family and friends, Johnson had a location, two students, and determination to continue with his school:

> I had neither money, nor rich friends, but it was laid on my heart to do something to assist moneyless young men to help themselves to get an education for the ministry of the pure gospel of Jesus Christ, our Lord. I had no money, but I had some experience as an author and preacher. I had many friends, but I found it impossible to enlist them, for I had never proven myself capable of managing the finances of such an institution as I

proposed to found. I was simply a voice, a very weak one, crying in the wilderness of poverty, doubt and uncertainty to my brethren to enter with me in a holy partnership with God to prepare and send into the fields . . . young men prepared in heart and mind to reap in the name of the Lord.[23]

Ashley Johnson, anxious to build his school but discouraged by a lack of resources, stood in the pulpit of the Bearden Christian Church in west Knox County on a Sunday in November, 1892, and sincerely told the congregation his desire to establish a school: "I am not seeking money. I am seeking encouragement. If the thing strikes you as possible, give me a word of encouragement." The service ended and the people filed out past Johnson and his wife without offering the encouragement he sought. As the Johnsons started to leave, William F. Crippen, a member of the congregation who had been baptized by Johnson, whispered in his ear: "Go ahead, and when you get started, I will give you one hundred dollars."[24] That was all the encouragement Johnson needed. He went home from the Bearden meeting and began to formulate more detailed plans, appealing to a friend in Georgia to supply blueprints for the main building. He announced his intentions to the brotherhood in the December 17, 1892 edition of the *Christian Standard*:

It will be modeled after the old "Schools of the Prophets" . . . . The chief part of the burden falls on me. I have labored hard, lived economically, and planned to do good with my accumulations, both of knowledge and money. I have a farm of 175 acres, and propose to give its proceeds . . . to the cause of Bible education—to prepare evangelists particularly for the South. . . . Tell the young men, particularly the poor and the struggling, about the new school.[25]

From a fireside in a cabin in South Carolina to a rustic pulpit in a country church, the spark had become a flame: Johnson Bible College was born. Its foundational pillars were already in place: a Bible-centered curriculum, evangelistic zeal, and concern for the "poor young man" with little opportunity. These principles would be refined in the future development of the School of the Evangelists.

Ashley and Emma Johnson shortly before the founding of the School of the Evangelists, c. 1890

Ashley and Emma Johnson after the founding of the School of Evangelists, c. 1898

The "White House" nearing completion, 1890

The Johnsons in a rare family portrait: (front row, left to right) James Sullivan, Jeremiah Crockett, Barbara; (back row) Charles Robert Lee, Jeremiah Crockett, George Washington, Ashley Sidney and Rufus Alexander.

Dr. and Mrs. Johnson with Archibald McLean, 1909 commencement speaker

"Showpup" with Ashley and Emma Johnson and her parents, Mr. and Mrs. J.D. Strawn, 1896

Ashley Johnson's parents, Crockett and Barbara Johnson

Dr. and Mrs. Johnson and "Showpup" overlooking the French Broad River and Johnson Island, c. 1896

The marriage of the Johnsons spanned 41 years and, in the words of Alva Ross Brown, was a "continual courtship."

Ashley and Emma Johnson's Twenty-fifth Wedding Anniversary Banquet, 1910

The story of the kissing oak is a beautiful account of the vibrant marriage of the Johnsons. As Dr. Johnson brought his bride to Knoxville for
the first time, he stopped the buggy by the giant oak which stood beside
Sevierville Pike, and they dismounted from the carriage. There they
kissed beside the oak and vowed never to carry a dispute past the tree.

From then on each time the Johnsons passed the tree Dr. Johnson
would stop the buggy and the Johnsons would kiss. The great tree came
to be known as the "kissing oak" throughout south Knox County. When
the motor car came along Dr. Johnson instructed the student drivers to
stop at the "kissing oak."

When the body of Dr. Johnson was returned to Kimberlin Heights after
his death in Baltimore in 1925, Mrs. Johnson kept her composure and
rode silently from the train station to the Heights. As her car passed the
oak, she broke down and wept.

The "kissing oak" eventually gave way to progress and the widening of
the road. Only a few today know where it stood, but for them it holds
special meaning.

Ripley's

Believe It or Not!

8-29

THE HUMAN DICTATING MACHINE

ASHLEY S. JOHNSON (1859-1925)
FOUNDER OF JOHNSON BIBLE
COLLEGE, KIMBERLIN HEIGHTS, TENN.,
*COULD COMPOSE 4 BUSINESS
LETTERS SIMULTANEOUSLY*
HE WOULD SIT FOR HOURS AT HIS
DESK WRITING LETTERS -- WHILE
DICTATING TO 3 SECRETARIES

On the road to Knoxville in the "Hack," 1908.

President Johnson and his automobile, 1915

President and Mrs. Johnson, 1918

President and Mrs. Johnson, Christmas 1923

Dr. Johnson in the college chapel, c. 1924

Emma Johnson at the graveside of Dr. Johnson with 1926 commencement speaker, W.H. Book

Original Main Building, c. 1895

"New" Main College Building, c. 1910

Cornerstone of the Main Building

President and Mrs. Johnson
with construction materials, 1905

Groundbreaking for new Main Building, 1905

Construction of the new Main Building, 1905

The Hill, c. 1900: Industrial Hall and Main Building

The Hill, c. 1980: Myrtle Hall, Alumni Chapel, gym/pool, Bell Hall, and Glass Library

Chapter 2
A Fulfilled Desire
1893–1925

At 8:30 on Friday morning, May 12, 1893, Captain Bruce Davis piloted his steamer Omega away from the docks in Knoxville and headed her upstream toward Kimberlin Heights. The approximately two hundred people on board were joined by others who boarded along the one and one-half hour, twelve-mile journey up the French Broad River. The boat was met upon its arrival by a large crowd of people who ushered the visitors up the river bank to the residence of Ashley S. Johnson, where a hearty "dinner on the ground" was shared by all. They assembled on the clearing on top of the hill overlooking the river for a simple ceremony marking the laying of the cornerstone for Johnson's new college, the School of the Evangelists.

After a prayer by Dr. Johnson, the Honorable Lewis Tillman, a lawyer from Knoxville and close friend of the Johnsons, delivered the address. Tillman candidly confessed that he was at first somewhat reluctant to take part in the ceremonies. He thought the enterprise was bound for failure and had discouraged Dr. Johnson from undertaking it. "But," Tillman continued, "now that he has made a start, I have changed my mind and believe this building will be completed and filled with students." After the completion of Tillman's address, Dr. Johnson briefly summarized his plans for the college, including a financial appeal to defray the cost of the main building. He replied to his friend's opening remarks: "Brother Tillman says that he has had it in his heart to discourage me. I declare in his presence that the man does not live who can discourage me. This is the Lord's work and I am determined to persevere until success or death."[2] Before Mr. Tillman returned to the Omega for the trip back to Knoxville he presented Dr. Johnson with the first book for the college's library: *A Life of Trust*. This small volume recounted the life and experiences of George Mueller, who had operated the great orphanages at Bristol, England, through prayer alone without ever having asked a human being for money—an appropriate word of inspiration for Ashley Johnson and his venture of faith. As dusk settled over the new "campus" Captain Davis steered his boat into the river's current for the return trip to Knoxville and the day that marked the founding of the School of the Evangelists drew to a close.

Ashley Johnson began the School of the Evangelists with three sincere convictions: preachers must be trained and sent to evangelize the world; a Bible-centered education was absolutely necessary to this training; and special opportunity must be given to the poor young man who desired to preach but could not afford an education. As the School of the Evangelists (the name was changed to Johnson Bible College in 1909) took shape, Johnson began to embody these convictions.

Drawing from the inspiration of the book Tillman had given them, the Johnsons dedicated the farm and the income from the sale of Ashley's books "to the Lord's work at Kimberlin Heights." Ashley wrote: "I soon discovered that I could not succeed in begging money even for so good a cause."[3] His first appeal letter in the spring of 1893 netted a grand total of thirty-five dollars! Out of this initial frustration the Johnsons developed a simple program for raising financial support—they first gave their own resources, then prayed fervently to God for income, and then made their needs known.

It was common for Johnson to write testimonies of how financial needs were miraculously supplied, such as the time he had borrowed $350 from a woman in the Kimberlin Heights community to erect a badly needed professor's house. The woman requested repayment at the end of the year but Johnson did not have it, nor was there much prospect of securing that sum of money. He went on a preaching tour of Texas and Oklahoma in hope of raising the money, but became seriously ill and was forced to return. One morning after his return, he was waiting for Mrs. Johnson to go to her classes and then planned to go to the bank and borrow the amount needed. Mrs.

Johnson handed him a stack of letters which he opened and discovered checks for $350, with which he promptly repaid his generous friend.[4]

In spite of the difficulties of securing financial support for the college, Johnson continued to build. The Main Building was completed by February, 1894. It was a three story frame structure containing a chapel, library, "recitation rooms," dormitory, dining room, and kitchen, and could accommodate approximately one hundred students. The School of the Evangelists opened on February 5 with four professors (Ashley and Emma Johnson, Albert Fitts, and Adam Adcock) and about forty students. Demonstrating his confidence in prayer, his own abilities, his students, and the worthiness of the project he had undertaken, Ashley Johnson laid the cornerstone for a second large building, Industrial Hall, only three months later on May 10, 1894.

As the main building was being constructed, Johnson came upon an idea that would become a central component of Johnson Bible College. E.A. Randall, a young carpenter from Michigan, had heard of the founding of the school and wrote Johnson, asking for an opportunity to earn an education by working on the main building. Johnson asked him to come and work, and then advertised for more workmen who would be willing to trade work for study. Randall and five other young men soon arrived on the Hill and Johnson's "industrial idea" was born. This was the way to provide for the poor young man.

The first catalog of the School of the Evangelists included a section on the "Industrial Department" in which Johnson appealed for twenty men experienced in gardening, poultry, and livestock management. From the inception of the work program Johnson understood the importance of teaching industry and thrift as well as academic subjects. Reflecting on the development of the industrial department, he wrote in 1921: "The first lesson we learned with these young fellows was that many of them needed to be trained to work."[5] The school was a social experiment, taking poor young men who had little personal discipline, moral guidance, and vocational training and providing character development along with their ministerial training. The work was not just to provide financial assistance—it was to shape lives by teaching responsibility. It offered "an op-

portunity for self-help to any young man who has only muscle
and a willingness to work to give in exchange for an education."[6] Johnson saw the work program as an essential facet of
his students' education. He was adamant in his convictions:

> If you are not willing to put your conscience into your work we
> do not want you under any circumstances. Laziness will not be
> tolerated. . . . Whenever a student, during work hours, stops to
> talk with everyone he may chance to meet, or stands or sits
> around, or if he fails to be at his place promptly, he will, without
> warning, lose his place. Now if you come here and after a few
> months we send you home, you will know who is to blame.[7]

His goal was to make the school ". . . a veritable bee-hive of industry and frugality."[8] A student entered the industrial department with full recognition of Dr. Johnson's terms:

> IF you are a wild, unsettled boy this is no place for you. We are
> not in the work of reforming bad boys, but in the work of devel-
> oping pious young men into preachers of the gospel.
> IF you are too lazy, or too "nice," or too sick to work, this is no
> place for you. This is not a charity. We can only give you a
> chance to earn an education and get it at the same time.[9]

This hard-work ethic was made both a condition for admission
and the means to refine the young men:

> We want parents and guardians . . . to understand that we occu-
> py high moral ground. . . . This Catalogue is not sent out to get
> students simply, but to "thin them." We want men of clean lives
> who will work and study, and we will keep no others. If you
> want to "eat, drink, swear, run about, have fun, and be a fool," I
> advise you to spend your money elsewhere. If you want to be a
> clean man and associate with clean men this is the place for you
> and we will welcome you.[10]

Johnson experimented often with his "industrial idea" and
several programs of "work-study" were developed. An example
of how the program worked is here taken from the 1906 catalog:

> I. TO THOSE WHO PAY: Ministerial and non-ministerial,
> $85.00 a year strictly in advance. No work required.
> II. TO THE INDUSTRIAL-MINISTERIAL STUDENT:
> $24.00 a year, strictly in advance; and 3 1/2 hours work daily

and 4 1/2 on Monday.

III. TO THE REGULAR FARM HAND: The young man who will come here September 19, 1906, and work regularly until June 1, 1907, can earn board, heated room, and plain washing while he works and receive in return two years schooling. No work required after schooling is earned.[11]

Reflecting a philosophy that charity should be offered in such a way that encouraged responsibility, the "industrial idea" was advertised as a self-help program "based on the hypothesis that to the full extent of his powers the student is to help himself."[12] No one was admitted to the Industrial Department who could feasibly pay his own way. Non-ministerial students were also excluded. Johnson's commitment was to provide the poor preacher boy with an education, and he stood by his promise that "no man has ever come to this school and found the door shut in his face on account of lack of money. We have a job for any boy who can furnish evidence of worthiness."[13]

It was obvious that "worthiness" meant a heart for evangelism, a head for learning, and a strong back. It also meant willingness to obey Johnson's authority. President Johnson declared his "College Platform" in the 1909 catalog: "Plank 1. You must do what I tell you, and do it in the manner I tell you, and do it right now; no argument, no questions, no substitutions, and do it right on, every day." Johnson was convinced that a lazy student would make a lazy preacher:

> The President of the School of the Evangelists "by nature and by grace" despiseth a loafer; . . . A preacher who loafs here will likely develop into a whittler of dry goods boxes on street corners and a village-preacher-gossip elsewhere—but he will not loaf here; that is certain![14]

Johnson's "boys" were primarily responsible for the expanding physical plant of the college. Although work was slow because of limited income, Industrial Hall was completed in 1898 and with the main building provided accommodations for 150 men. By 1903 a dairy barn, granary, shop, bakery, boiler house, summer kitchen, and cannery had been added. An additional 250 acres of farmland had also been secured.[15] All of these enterprises were manned by work students under the careful supervision of the president. Ashley Johnson was proud of his farm and the way his boys worked it. Most of the young men had no opportunity to pursue an education without the financial assistance offered through the work-study program. It was an excellent example of how to extend needed assistance without demeaning the self-esteem or minimizing the responsibility of the recipient.

One cannot mention the farm without reference to Johnson's prize cattle, the Dixie Holstein Herd. In the summer of 1903, Johnson decided that his small herd of Jerseys was inadequate to meet the increasing dairy needs of the college. He sold the entire herd and invested the proceeds, along with other gifts to the college, in a small herd of fifteen Holsteins (in Johnson's words: "those big milk machines").[16] These developed into one of the finest herds in the South, producing more than enough dairy products for the college and earning the college great notoriety for its champion animals. Johnson often claimed that the only endowment that Johnson Bible College had was "the Lord and a herd of Holstein cows."[17] Ashley Johnson appreciated his cows: "When faith gets tired I often go to the dairy barn and walk among and talk to the great cows, one of whom gave 71 gallons of milk and made 25 pounds of butter in seven days, and I always come away refreshed and encouraged." Many Johnson Bible College students worked their way through school tending, milking, and cleaning up after cattle. Percy Cross reported his visit to the campus in 1913 to the *Christian Standard* and noted:

> It was an inspiring scene to see those embryo preachers milking those cows and making butter. . . . We saw a half-dozen more going-to-be preachers loading fertilizer wagons from a rank heap of the same, laughing and singing "Stepping in the Light." Brother Cross shouted, "You fellows are all right." Their response: "Amen, Brother Cross; we're going to be preachers some day. This is just a part of the training."[18]

As important as the industrial idea may have been, it was secondary to the overriding purpose of the School of the Evangelists: to train preachers of the gospel of Jesus Christ. From its inception, Ashley Johnson's college was a special purpose institution with a single aim: "We want it distinctly understood

that this school is for the training of young men to preach, and
not for anybody else."[19] Dr. Johnson reiterated this purpose re-
peatedly in nearly every official communication from the college, and devoted his life to its objective: "The one
overwhelming, persistent, resistless desire of my heart and de-
sign of the college of which by God's grace I founded and of
which I have been president for twenty-seven years, is to train
preachers."[20] Johnson's admission policy required a statement
from the student that his desire was to become a preacher—"I
cannot afford to trifle my time away with young men who have
no purpose."[21] One of Johnson's early mottos was "A Preacher-
Training Institution in a Preacher-Growing Atmosphere." Although programs were made available for non-ministerial
students, enrollment was limited and often discouraged by
President Johnson. It has already been noted that non-ministerial students were not allowed to work in the industrial department. His policy was clearly stated:

We run this School for the purpose of training preachers. We do
not seek any other kind of students. Every young man who
comes here must solemnly pledge himself to this end or pay
$150.00 (in advance) a year as a non-ministerial student until
he makes up his mind. If a young man comes here to make a
preacher and changes his mind, we expect him to leave at once
and give some one else the chance. All our propositions are
made with this understanding.[22]

One could not train preachers, however, without a strong
commitment to the Bible as the Word of God or thorough
knowledge of that Word. Johnson's "Plea" was:

Preach the Word—preach it plainly, only, earnestly, persistent-
ly, movingly—do not preach anything else.
. . . Philosophical dissertations, pretty essays, lectures, enter-
tainments and a dry baptistery [sic] are co-existent and parallel.
Again, I say: Preach the Word."[23]

President Johnson reflected the strong commitment to the
authority of the Bible that was central to the Restoration
Movement. He was heavily influenced by the writings of
Alexander Campbell and the principles of his movement: "We
stand for the old Book, the whole Book without supplement,

amendment, or theory of any kind, ancient or modern."[24] Johnson stated "The Religious Position of Johnson Bible College" in reference to the Bible:

> This institution stands for the Bible, in the sense that we believe that it is the inspired word of God as our fathers believed it. We believe that holy men of God spoke as they were moved by the Holy Spirit in olden times. . . . We believe in the inspiration and authority of the sacred scriptures, and by these we stand or fall. . . . the Bible and the Bible alone is the religion of the Protestants and particularly that part of them who congregate at Johnson Bible College.[25]

A young professor from the college, Robert M. Bell, wrote to the *Christian Standard* in 1920:

> The teacher who questions the Bible as the only revealed word of God and Jesus Christ as His only begotten Son has about as much chance getting into Johnson Bible College as the ex-Kaiser has of getting into the British Parliament. Everybody knows just where J.B.C. stands on all the fundamentals.[26]

These convictions were embodied within the curriculum of the college: "We believe that the study of the Bible is of paramount and supreme importance to the preacher and offer about one-fourth of our College work in its study."[27] One must note, however, that the curriculum also consisted of a great variety of courses. Johnson's program included a liberal arts course of study in addition to the Bible work and reflected Alexander Campbell's early curriculum at Bethany College. The liberal arts courses, however, were subservient to the Bible course:

> We propose to give our boys a good English and Classical education, but all these things are tributary to and subservient to the one greater end: a good—indeed the best—Bible education. We teach English, Mathematics, Science, Latin and Greek, History, only because of their value to the mind and as a supplement to our Bible work. We do not discount scholarship, but emphasize the one vast, unsatisfied and all prevailing need of Bible scholarship.[28]

> Our motto is: "Thorough work in every branch by everybody," but—mark it well—we count a man a failure as a preacher and

would blush to own him as our "son in the gospel," who would go forth from these halls better prepared to preach Science, History, Philosophy, than the old Jerusalem gospel![29]

From its founding the school consisted of the Preparatory Department or Academy for students who had no secondary education and the college proper.[30] The Academy offered basic arithmetic, grammar, spelling, reading, history, and geography courses. By 1902 this program had developed into a clearly defined two-year course and included advanced math courses such as algebra, geometry, and trigonometry, as well as rhetoric, sociology, physiology, civics, and Latin. The Academy was expanded into a four-year program by 1903 because so many students lacked any high school education. Although there was much "tinkering" with this department, it generally offered either a complete secondary education to those who needed it, or a college preparatory for those who needed remedial assistance in certain areas. As the community on the Hill expanded, the Academy also provided secondary education for the children of faculty, staff, and Kimberlin Heights neighbors.

Ashley Johnson certainly wanted to focus on more advanced college work, but he recognized the educational levels of his constituency. The Academy was an integral part of the school and few distinctions were made between its students and those who were enrolled in the college proper. It was not until 1909 (when the school's name was changed) that the Academy curriculum was listed separately in the catalog from that of the college.

The earliest college curriculum available (1896) consisted of the following courses:

Freshman:
    Faith Development
    Geography
    Arithmetic
    Grammar
    Word Lessons
    English

Sophomore:
    Bible
    Faith Development
    Algebra
    English
    History

Junior:
    Bible
    Faith Development

Senior:
    Bible
    Faith Development

English
Physical Geography
Rhetoric
Ancient Geography
Physiology and Hygiene

Church History
Political Economy
Psychology and Logic
Moral Philosophy

It is of interest to note that no formal theology or homiletics courses were included. By 1900, however, the curriculum included four years of "Theory and Practice of Preaching" which were incorporated into Dr. Johnson's Epistles class.

Under President Johnson's tenure the college curriculum settled into two basic programs of study: the English-Bible Course (Bachelor of Literature) and the Classical-Bible Course (Bachelor of Arts). The latter required a more stringent preparatory education (including two years of Latin), one year of Latin at the college level, and two (or even three) years of Greek. The 1925-26 Catalog outlined the following courses for the Bachelor of Arts degree:

FRESHMAN

First Semester

Pentateuch and Bible Geography
English
Oriental History in Bible Times
Astronomy
Logic

Second Semester

History of Israel
Geography of Israel
History
Geology
Common Objections to
        Christianity

SOPHOMORE

History and Geography of Israel
Homiletics
Sociology
Chemistry
Greek I
Public Speaking

Prophets
Pastoral Theology
School Administration
Economics
Chemistry
Greek I
Public Speaking

JUNIOR

Gospels
Greek II
College English
Comparative Religions
Church History

Gospels
Greek II
College English
History of the
        Restoration Movement
Church History

SENIOR

Acts and Epistles	Epistles
Theology	Theology
Evidences of Christianity	Evidences of Christianity
Philosophy	Philosophy
Psychology	Psychology

These two basic options were offered in a variety of programs which changed often. By 1922 the college was offering five courses of study: Bachelor of Arts, which was considered the normal ministerial course; Bachelor of Literature, the basic English-Bible course which was also offered to non-ministerial students; Certificates in Bible-English-History (three years) or Bible-English, for students who had already completed college work elsewhere; and a Certificate in Bible, a one-year course "especially for older men."[31] The college irregularly offered Master of Theology (one year beyond the Bachelor of Arts), Master of Arts (apparently the same as the M.Th.), and Bachelor of Divinity (a three year Greek-English course which assumed some college transfer work) degrees. President Johnson continued to upgrade the quality of his program and was especially proud when one of his graduates was admitted to the University of Michigan Graduate School without conditions. This prompted him to declare, "Last year we equalized our academy and college work with the great University of Michigan: Johnson Bible College and Johnson boys are coming into their own."[32]

The few surviving class notes from the early years of the School of the Evangelists suggest that the Correspondence Bible School lessons along with Dr. Johnson's *Self-Interpreting New Testament* and *Condensed Biblical Cyclopedia* provided the course content. Ashley Johnson's theological training had consisted of reading the Bible for himself with little additional commentary. President and Mrs. Johnson (who had taken some classes at Hamilton College, Ontario, but was trained in Bible by her husband during the C.B.C. years) taught most of the Bible classes. The 1902 catalog outlined their teaching duties: in the first two years of the program President Johnson taught the Pentateuch while Mrs. Johnson taught the remainder of the Old Testament, the Gospels, and Acts. Dr. Johnson then took the Juniors and Seniors through the remainder of the New Testament.

Albert Fitts and John Dickson, two of the early faculty members, had been trained by Dr. Johnson, although Fitts later (1909) graduated from Drake University. Robert Black was certainly correct in his appraisal of the early faculty of the school: "It is evident that the faculty in the beginning was composed largely of 'home talent.' "[33] However difficult it was to attract (and especially pay) qualified faculty members, one can trace a gradual positive development. By 1915 there were two men with Master of Arts and two others with Bachelor of Arts degrees to complement Dr. and Mrs. Johnson's twenty years of teaching experience. President Johnson also utilized upperclassmen as teachers in the Academy. The 1924-25 catalog listed five "Student Teachers" along with the regular faculty, administration, and staff of the college.

The faculty member of the college under Ashley S. Johnson was required to teach a wide variety of subjects. Specialization in a particular field, if not unknown, was impractical at the school. William H. Sperry, faculty member from 1917-1931 and Dean of the college for the last four years of his J.B.C. career, listed his teaching responsibilities: Church History, Restoration Movement, Comparative Religions, Philosophy, Philosophy of the Christian Religion, Greek New Testament, Latin New Testament, Astronomy, Geology, Psychology, Chemistry, Ethics, and Missions.[34] In spite of laboring under such difficult academic obstacles, Dean Sperry was impressed by the accomplishments of the college's program:

> Visitors at JBC were constantly surprised that instead of a sort of hill-school to help lads learn to barely read and write, our students were discussing Philosophy, Languages, Mathematics and most other college subjects the same as in any other standard college.[35]

The first decade of Johnson's School of the Evangelists witnessed slow but steady growth. From its first class of 42 students, enrollment grew to a high of 144 students in 1898 and an average of 92 pupils per year. There were fifty-six graduates by 1904. These students came from at least twenty different states and three foreign countries. As has been noted, the physical plant also increased with the Main Building and

Industrial Hall serving as the primary educational and living facilities along with numerous support buildings for the college and the farm. An alumni association was formed in 1900 to encourage support of the college. J.C. Coggins, the first graduate of the C.B.C., wrote the *Christian Standard* in 1901 to laud Johnson's accomplishments: "He now claims a family of over a thousand young preachers, in which I have the honor of being his first-born son. He put it into my heart to preach."[36] The school was incorporated under the laws of the State of Tennessee in 1901. Ashley Johnson himself seemed to sense that his venture had outgrown its infancy and was now on more solid ground. He wrote to the *Standard,*

> I have done all that I can do. The struggle has been long and hard. Like the burning bush, it has frequently appeared that the work would be consumed by its own poverty. Probably there has not been a time in five years in which I have not been required to put up my good name to procure groceries to supply the young men with the bare necessities of life. . . . I have for ten years been in the fight for the poor boy who wishes to preach the gospel. I am growing gray-headed in the struggle, but I have only begun to fight.[37]

Johnson had built his school in spite of discouragement, poverty, fire, and flood, but the most threatening storm in the life of the college was on the horizon. On Thursday, December 1, 1904, while President Johnson was conducting a revival meeting at Alexandria, Indiana, a fire consumed the uninsured Main Building. Starting from a defective flue, the fire spread quickly throughout the large frame building and by nightfall reduced it to ashes. A bucket brigade organized by the students heroically saved the other buildings, including Industrial Hall. Dr. Johnson was immediately notified by telegraph and assured that the 117 "boys" had secured other lodgings for the night and were awaiting his arrival. About 10:30 the next morning Dr. Johnson's telegram to his wife brought this reply: "Cheer up sweetheart; God reigns. The School of Evangelists lives and will live. Home tomorrow." He later wired Professor Pierce: "Let the Heights be glad. The word fail is foreign to His eternal purpose in us. Amen! Never felt so much like going on. Hold the boys till I come."[38]

Dr. Johnson arrived on Sunday afternoon. As he came within sight of the college, the students lined the walk in front of the White House and sang, "My Faith Looks Up to Thee." Johnson conducted a communion service on the veranda of the house and then led a prayer meeting that evening in the upper hall of Industrial Hall. He suspended the college and promised his boys that supper would be ready for them in the basement of the new building on December 1, 1905. As proof of his word, Ashley Johnson conveyed the message that before leaving Indiana he had secured two thousand dollars from benefactor Joseph Irwin to begin the rebuilding. He wrote the *Christian Standard*:

> We are not discouraged. Our faith in God is stronger than ever. The gospel must be preached to the whole creation. The open door before the poor young man who desires above every other desire to preach, so rudely closed, must and shall be opened again.[39]

The cornerstone for a new twenty-five thousand dollar brick building (now called Old Main) was laid on May 12, 1905. Johnson's promise to feed the boys supper was postponed only five weeks—the new building opened on January 11, 1906. It was described as "two buildings in one": the front part containing chapel, reception room, five recitation rooms, and three society halls; the rear of the building, divided from the main part by a solid brick wall, was a three story dormitory with accommodations for ninety-six students and a basement for the dining room and kitchen. Johnson sent notice of the opening of the new building to the *Christian Standard* and described the marker which would, above all others, identify the character of Johnson Bible College: "On a beautiful slab of Tennessee marble near the front door of the Main Building, we have chiseled these words: 'Open Day and Night to the Poor Young Man Who Desires, Above Every Other Desire, to Preach the Gospel of Christ.' "[40]

The "catastrophe" had turned into a stepping stone for an era of tremendous growth in the college's facilities. By 1914 the campus consisted of the Main Building, the president's home (the White House), Industrial Hall, the Gymnasium (1908), Irwin Library (1912), three professor's houses, and the support buildings for the operation of the school and farm. The Taber Chemical Laboratory was added in 1924 along with two more houses for professors.

In 1909 the students presented a petition to President Johnson requesting a change in the name of the college from School of the Evangelists to Johnson Bible College. They argued that the institution had outgrown the name "School" and should be recognized as a college "just as other schools doing the same work." Since Ashley and Emma Johnson had given their life's work to the college and the work was "indissolubly associated" with their name, the President "bowed to the inevitable" and appealed to the Board of Directors to approve the change. In the notice of the change of name in the 1909-10 catalog, Dr. Johnson made it clear that it would not alter the purpose or character of the institution: "We have been and we are doing college work—both classical and English—and we expect to enlarge constantly, but: Never to get beyond that which is on record in the Book."[41]

The two decades between the fire and the death of President Johnson in 1925 saw encouraging growth in the number of students, graduates, college facilities, and financial base. There were 78 students who returned to the resumption of classes in the new building in January, 1906. Enrollment quickly increased to 110 in the fall term and to 188 in 1910. Ashley Johnson declared 1911 to be "the best year in our history" and enrollment averaged over 150 students per year until the war years of 1918-19. There were 3879 students enrolled and 200 graduates during Ashley Johnson's years as president (1893-1925). These students came from over thirty different states (although the largest percentage came from the upper South and the Midwest) and at least eight foreign countries (Armenia, Canada, Greece, Kurdistan (Persia), Poland, Puerto Rico, Russia, and Turkey).

Most of the students, of course, were single males between the ages of seventeen and twenty-seven (these age parameters were President Johnson's official policy, but one would assume that many exceptions were made). Dr. Johnson at first discouraged married men but later admitted that he "could make special exceptions with proper recommendations."[42] He gave notice in 1907 that he would make room for three or four cou-

ples with no children ("or at most not over one").[43] He strictly
ordered his "boys" to "leave your love affairs behind; we have
seen many promising young men fail because of such affairs."[44]
Women were obviously present on campus, however, and par-
ticipated in many of the college activities. The 1919 catalog includes pictures of women in the College Orchestra, Tennis
Club, and Timothy Club. One photograph of a group of females
was entitled "The Co-eds—Local and Young Preacher's Wives."
One can assume that most campus women were married to faculty, staff, or students, but there were a few single females enrolled in the Academy.

The college academic calendar followed the quarter system
until 1915, when it was converted to semesters. The calendar
for 1903-04 was as follows:

September 22	Fall term opens
September 27	Convocation
November 26	Thanksgiving Service and Senior Class Orations
December 11-12	Fall term exams
December 15	Winter term opens
December 25	Christmas vacation
February 1	Mid-term exams
February 22	Junior Class Orations
March 4-5	Winter term exams
March 8	Spring term opens
April 11	Sophomore Class Orations
April 18	Mid-term exams
May 2	Orational Contests
May 21	Entertainment by Literary Societies
May 22	Baccalaureate Service
May 23-24	Spring term exams
May 23	Class Day
May 24	Literary Address
May 25	Commencement

The students were rarely away from campus during the
school year and many stayed to work for the summer as well.
There were no Thanksgiving or Christmas vacations, and only
one or two days between terms. The difficulty of securing
transportation was the primary reason for the lack of "breaks."

Students normally worked three and one-half hours per day,
six days per week. Those who had to work on Sunday to main-

tain the farm were allowed Monday off. It appears that from the beginning of the school there were no classes on Monday to accommodate those who preached and traveled to area churches on Sunday and could not return until the following day. Classes began at 7:00 A.M. (although the work day started an hour or two earlier) and continued into the evening. The compulsory evening prayer meeting was held every night at 7:30. Students retired to their dormitory early (especially before the advent of electricity in the new Main Building) with the exception of an occasional literary society meeting.

As in colleges today, one of the most important concerns of the students (and President Johnson himself, judging from the constant references in the catalogs) was the food. Dr. Johnson was unsympathetically honest about what the prospective student would find in the dining hall: "Our fare is characterized by two things, plentifulness, plainness."[45] Most of the food was produced right on the farm and, again in Dr. Johnson's words, was "plain and wholesome." He warned the student: "If you are not willing to live on this without grumbling, we advise you to stay home or go elsewhere."[46] He continued:

> If you think more of your stomach than you do of the Master, this is no place for you. . . . A young man came here recently and did not like it because it did not look like home! Of course not— "there is no place like home," and if you expect to still be a baby you would do well to stay there! Our forefathers lived on plain food and fought for their country; surely we can live on it and work for an education in order to preach the "glorious gospel!"[47]

Dr. Howard E. Short recounted his days as a student at J.B.C. in the mid-1920s and made reference to the menu:

> The food was a little monotonous: biscuits and milk gravy for breakfast this morning; biscuits and corn syrup ("Zip") tomorrow. Navy beans for lunch and boiled potatoes for supper; tomorrow they will be reversed. Apple pie tonight; sweet potato pie tomorrow.[48]

There was almost no meat served (except on special occasions) and the primary bill of fare was beans, beans, and more beans (Dr. Johnson claimed to have used twenty-five bushels of Navy beans for the 1904-05 school year)! One student suggested that the "B" in the college initials stood for "Beans," not "Bible!" After explaining the plainness of the food to a visitor, President Johnson proudly observed: "It has been nearly four years since we threw open our doors, and we have never had a death in the building and very little sickness. The young men nearly all gain greatly in weight, which proves that our fare is good for them."[49]

The isolation of the college (and some would argue the all-male population) fostered limited extra-curricular activities for the students. Dr. Johnson warned his students in the college catalog:

> The social life of the institution is what the students and teachers make it. We are on a farm of 250 acres, twelve miles from the city. The society here is good, if faith in God and high purpose count for anything, but society as ordinarily defined is unknown on Kimberlin Heights.[50]

The chief entertainment was in the literary societies—Johnsonian, Kimberlinian, Alethian, Robinsonian, Errett, Chapman, Philodelphian—which encouraged poetry reading, musical concerts, debates, dramatic presentations, and orations. Every student was required to be a member of a literary society. Basketball, baseball, tennis, and track were popular sports and competition between classes was often heated.

Insight into college life may be gleaned from a report to the *Christian Standard* on the November 26, 1909 Thanksgiving Day activities. The morning began with chapel which included a Thanksgiving sermon by Professor Pierce. This was followed by a large dinner "arranged and prepared" by President and Mrs. Johnson. The "boys" were joined for the day by the champions of the Knox City Basketball League, the YMCA Tigers, who came with a crowd of supporters "to sample our food and test our mettle." The outcome was not good for the home team: "At the end of one of the hardest contested games ever played at J.B.C. the score stood 20 to 19 in favor of the Tigers." The senior class delivered orations to the rest of the student body in the evening as the big day came to a close.[51]

The student who came to Johnson Bible College pledged himself to obey the rules of the school. Dr. Johnson insisted that the only rule for the college was "Be a gentleman and a

Christian," but then followed that principle with a lengthy list of regulations! He was especially against "tobacco in any form" and damage of the college buildings. He subtly suggested that any violation of the college rules would "subject the offender to an invitation to a faculty meeting." He compared the institution to West Point Military Academy: "Shall we not set up a high standard of personal honor for the soldiers of the King?"[52] Each student had to sign a matriculation pledge of which the following is an example from the 1898-99 school term:

Matriculation Obligation

In order to become a student of the School of the Evangelists for the year 1898-99, I have affixed my name to the following obligation which I promise, God being my helper, to respect at all times and under all circumstances to the best of my ability:

I. I will regard myself as a full partner in the work.

II. I will "keep off the grass" and refrain from making paths anywhere on the place, campus or farm.

III. To take good care of my room, clean it up early in the morning, be careful of the furniture and to report and pay for all damages done by me to buildings or furniture.

IV. Not to use my window-sill as a wash stand, throw water or paper out at the windows, or otherwise pollute the buildings or grounds, and also not to carry mud on my feet into the buildings.

V. To see that the Electric Light in my room is promptly turned out during prayer meeting and during all other times when not absolutely needed.

VI. Not to rest my feet on the window sill or to indulge in any scuffling, running or other boisterous conduct in the Dining Room, in the Halls, on the Porches or in any other part of the buildings.

VII. Not to drive nails or tacks in the buildings, nor lounge on my bed during the day unless I am too sick to stay up. . . .

IX. Not to trespass on the orchards or gardens, or to partake of any food or food material belonging to the School until it is cooked and put on the tables—at regular meal time—in the Dining Room. . . .

XIII. Not to leave the grounds for a meal or any other purpose—except to go to the neighborhood stores on personal business—without permission of the President.

XIV. To be regular and prompt in attendance to all my classes, my Literary Society and the House of God and to the best of my ability bear my part.

XV. Not to keep matches in my room except in metal cases, not to have a lamp or any other light except a candles (sic) save in cases of sickness and then by express permission of the President.

XVI. Not to introduce or indulge in any argument or contention among the students that will produce strife, and to conscientiously and faithfully attend to my duty in whatever position I am placed, without fear or favor.

XVII. To stand by the right always as God gives me light to see it, and to try to purge myself of "all filthiness of the flesh and spirit" and try to remember always that I am my brother's keeper.

[Signed]   F.J. Wobler, Payne, Ohio

            H.M. Chinigeorgian, Massovan, Turkey

            F.H. Giezentanner, Bearden, Tennessee[53]

Two overriding concerns of Ashley Johnson, evangelism and prayer, were also an integral part of life at the college in the first three decades. It is difficult to convey the intensity of Ashley Johnson's convictions about both. From the day of his conversion he was wholeheartedly convinced that the preaching of the gospel to every creature was the foremost duty of every Christian. His writings were filled with lofty rhetoric in which he attempted to communicate the depth of his convictions:

> There can be but one conclusion—the one all-prevailing, overwhelming, ever-present, ever-crying obligation of the individual Christian . . . is to use his body, his time, his talent, his influence, his money, to see that the gospel is preached in its glorious provision and apostolic simplicity to this generation.[54]

Johnson's priorities reflected his evangelistic fervor: "The preaching of the gospel to every creature is vital, paramount, pressing, and every other question agitating the minds of men is utterly insignificant and little and mean when compared to it."[55]

This zeal for preaching the gospel was complemented by his unwavering commitment to prayer. Deeply influenced by the biography of George Mueller, *A Life of Trust*, Dr. Johnson devoted his life to the "school of prayer." Prayer meetings were held daily on the campus and an "Upper Room" was set aside for the purpose of prayer in the Main Building. Alva Ross Brown's eloquent tribute to Ashley Johnson's commitment to prayer conveys the intensity of this quality in his life:

Great in intellect! Great in faith! Great in spiritual passion!
Great as teacher, preacher, writer, organizer, and executive!
But President Ashley S. Johnson was not greatest as any one of
these. He was most sublime when he prayed! . . . His effect on
others was unspeakable. Said Prof. E.L. Barham: "When I heard
him pray I knew that I was in the presence of a man who lived
nearer to God than any man I had ever heard before." And
Archibald McLean declared in characteristic brief utterance,
"Not one man in a million can pray like Brother Johnson." His
prayers searched the hearts of men. There were times when
one's blood pulsated violently, when tears forced their way to
the eyes, when a desire to cry out in ecstacy had to be choked.
. . . It is worth the efforts of a lifetime to learn to pray as this
man did.[56]

Johnson's concern for prayer was embodied in his oft-repeat-
ed slogan:

We work as if everything depends upon work;
We trust as if everything depends upon trust;
We believe as if everything depends upon faith;
We pray as if everything depends upon prayer;
We wait as if everything depends upon waiting.[57]

This passage has been modified into the current motto of the
college: "Faith, Prayer, Work."

Ashley Johnson stood behind the pulpit in the chapel of the
Main Building on Monday, January 4, 1925, during the
evening prayer meeting with his students. He was to leave the
next day for the Baltimore Sanitarium and an appointment
with Dr. Howard A. Kelly who had assured the Johnsons that
he could provide relief for Ashley's suffering from frequently
occurring severe headaches. It was to be the last address to his
"boys." Commenting on never returning to Kimberlin Heights
but going on to heaven, Johnson declared, "When I arrive, I
will say, I am Ashley Sidney Johnson from Kimberlin
Heights—and so this is the New Jerusalem!" Broken with emo-
tion, President Johnson wept as he pronounced a benediction
upon those gathered that evening on the Hill: "God Almighty
bless you! God Almighty keep you! God Almighty bring you up
at last to the Golden Gates!"[58]

Ashley Johnson died in Baltimore eleven days later of a
cerebral hemorrhage. Mrs. Johnson returned with the body for

the funeral which was held on Sunday afternoon, January 18. After two hymns, "The Unclouded Day" and "Nearer My God to Thee," and addresses by Dr. H.A. Morgan, President of the University of Tennessee, and Dr. Ritchie Ware, minister of Knoxville's Fifth Avenue Christian Church, Johnson's body was laid in the ground under the shadow of the Main Building and the Prayer Oak. "The father of the poor, young ministerial student and . . . great champion of New Testament Christianity" had been called home.[59]

One may wonder if this is a history of Johnson Bible College or a biography of Ashley S. Johnson. One cannot draw a distinction between the two. The character and success of the School of the Evangelists depended solely upon the indefatigable zeal and determination of Ashley S. Johnson. This is not to discount the sacrifice and invaluable contributions of others. But one cannot examine the various historical sources without being impressed with the faith, fixity of purpose, and persistence of this man. Perhaps in anticipation that he would not see another school term, President Johnson had written in the 1924-25 college catalog: "The founder has controlled the institution from the beginning and he has so arranged the deed and trust fund that his principles, his faith, and his ideals will control it for ages."[60] The vision Ashley Johnson saw fulfilled in the School of the Evangelists and Johnson Bible College would continue in his wife, Emma, and young son in the faith Alva Ross Brown.

The Gymnasium, dedicated 1908

Taber Chemistry Laboratory, dedicated 1924

Emma E. Johnson Industrial Hall (Old Dusty), 1894

Irwin Library, dedicated 1912

Teacher Training Class, 1906; J.A. Lord, editor of Christian Standard with Prof. Martin Pierce in center

The first chapel in the original Main Building

The kitchen in the new Main Building

The old summer kitchen, c. 1900

The view from Sunset Hill, c. 1900

The library was housed across from the chapel room in the Main Building before Irwin Library was built in 1912.

The college chapel in the Main Building

The Prayer Oak

Prayer Room in Main Building, 1926

The "baptizing hole" in the French Broad River

The farm road up the Hill, c. 1915

Baseball game in the field below the Hill, c. 1910

The steamboat "Annabell King" docking at Kimberlin Heights, 1911

"Professors Row," 1922

The White House, barn and farm buildings viewed from the top of the Main Building, 1926

The barge crossing the French Broad River to Johnson Island, 1926

JBC Faculty, 1914

Professor and Mrs. Martin Pierce, Mr. Stevenson, Dr. and Mrs. Johnson, 1908

W.F. Crippen, donor of the first $100 for the School of the Evangelists

James I. Robinson, "Uncle Jim" — generous encourager of Ashley Johnson

Albert T. Fitts, first graduate of the School of the Evangelists

Konstantin Jaroshevich, class of 1916, missionary to Poland

The first student body, 1893

Eighth Grade Class, 1923

JBC student Walter G. Smith preaching at prayer meeting, 1916

Men ordained to the ministry by Dr. Johnson, 1923

E.I. Osgood Missions Rally in chapel, 1906

JBC Band, 1919

Kimberlinian Literary Society, 1909

The "Blue Birds" (1916–17), Tennis Club (1922–23) and baseball team (1911–12)

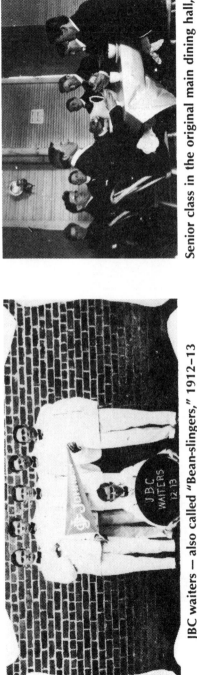

Senior class in the original main dining hall, 1904

Room in men's dormitory, 1910

JBC waiters — also called "Bean-slingers," 1912–13

Founder's Day parade, May 12, 1914

Ashley Johnson and one of his prize Holsteins, 1903

The coal train going to the railroad depot for the annual coal supply, 1910

The laundry in the boiler house built in 1905

Putting up hay, 1923

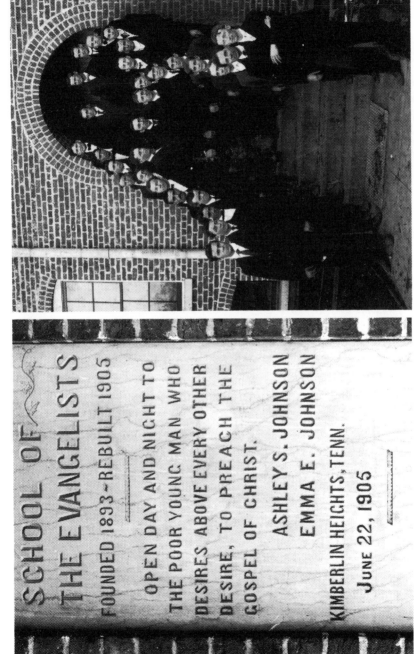

Robinsonian Literary Society, 1907

Marble marker at the doorway of the Main Building

Funeral procession for Ashley S. Johnson with teachers and seniors carrying casket and following, 1925

Mrs. Ashley S. (Emma) Johnson beside her husband's grave in front of the Main Building, 1926

Chapter 3
An Undaunted Desire
1925–1941

On October 22, 1927, twenty-two year old Alva Ross Brown sat in the office where he had served as "assistant" to Ashley and Emma Johnson since 1923 and wrote an impassioned letter to the "Beloved Old Guard"—faithful alumni and supporters of Johnson Bible College. This time, however, the "assistant" was writing as the president of the college. Mrs. Johnson had followed her husband in death on May 30 of that year and had announced one week earlier that young Brown would succeed her. His letter simply announced the opening of the 1927-28 school term and subtly mentioned two items that would haunt his presidency: he had imposed on the "business friends" of the college to "carry the bills" while he attempted to raise ten thousand dollars, and he had "pleaded with the boys to be unanimous in their moral and spiritual support" of his leadership.[1] The stress to overcome these formidable obstacles—economic hardship and opposition from some within the college's constituency—would hinder the physical growth of the institution and, some would say, send Alva Ross Brown to an early grave.

Emma Elizabeth Strawn Johnson was well qualified to succeed her husband as President of Johnson Bible College after his death in January, 1925. She had left her family in Grimsby Park, Ontario, Canada, and followed Ashley Johnson to the southern United States after their marriage in 1884 and had been a full partner in both the Correspondence Bible College and the School of the Evangelists (Johnson Bible College). Even though she had completed only a few courses of college work, Mrs. Johnson proved to be an intelligent and capable teacher of the sophomore and senior Bible classes. She served officially as college treasurer, registrar, bookkeeper, hostess, and pianist, and unofficially as "preceptress to the young men in the art of cultured behavior."[2] Even though her quiet, unassuming personality often kept her in the background, no one questioned her significant contribution to the college. In fact, she had assumed most of the presidential duties of her husband for the last ten years of his life because of his recurring illness. There was no doubt that she would become the next president of Johnson Bible College.

Although Mrs. Johnson immediately poured herself into the responsibilities of the office, it was apparent that she was limited by her own failing health. She had major cancer surgery in 1923 and lived in fear of its return. No stranger to the daily administration of the college, she continued the program with few problems, even initiating plans for a new building. Mrs. Johnson soon persuaded Albert T. Fitts to return to the college to teach the Bible courses and greatly respected his counsel as well as that of Dean Sperry. She became increasingly dependent, however, upon her young assistant who was soon to graduate and leave for further studies at the University of Michigan.

Alva Ross Brown was born September 7, 1905 in Fairfield, Pennsylvania. After graduating from high school in 1922 (at age sixteen, with high honors), he came to Johnson Bible College as a promising student. Somewhat "bookish," Brown excelled in the classroom—Professor Robert M. Bell later declared that of the four thousand students he had taught, "only two or three were as good, but none better."[3] Brown also had received solid spiritual training at an early age, having been baptized by Henry F. Loos, a prominent preacher and leader within the Restoration Movement. Brown's talent was recognized by the Johnsons, who secured him as their office assistant in 1923 and also appointed him to teach mathematics in the Academy. He was ordained to the Christian ministry by Ashley Johnson in May, 1924, continued to work in the President's office, and was soon an integral part of the "inner circle" of the college administration. The Johnsons, whose only child had died as an infant in 1891, spoke affectionately of Alva Ross, often addressing him in correspondence as "our dear son

Alva." Brown obviously held the same warmth toward them, referring to himself as "your boy" and "lovingly your son."[4] It soon appeared that this young "son in the faith" was being groomed by the Johnsons for future leadership in the college. After graduation from the college in 1926, Brown enrolled in the graduate school of the University of Michigan and completed a Master of Arts degree in one year.

During the summer of 1926 Mrs. Johnson began to experience severe pain in her right shoulder and an examination revealed that her cancer had recurred. Given only a few months to live, she went to her husband's surgeon, Dr. Kelly, in Baltimore for treatment but received little encouragement. By spring of 1927 her condition had worsened. Early in the morning on May 30 she sent for Dean Sperry and his wife and exhorted them to be faithful to the college's work. A few hours later, in the words of Alva Ross Brown, "she entered into rest" at age sixty-four.[5] The memorial service was held on June 2 in the college chapel with William Sperry preaching the funeral sermon. Her body was placed by the side of her companion in the quiet grove on the hillside. The Johnson era at the college had ended.

The question that had been considered for some time by alumni and friends of Johnson Bible College now came to the forefront: who would become the next president of Johnson Bible College? Another question was asked by the more skeptical: can Johnson Bible College continue to exist without Ashley and Emma Johnson? The college had faced crises before, but none of this magnitude. Alva Ross Brown, who now found himself in the middle of the debate, expressed what was on the mind of those familiar with the college:

> Johnson Bible College has experienced its supreme shock. In less than three years Mrs. Johnson has followed her husband into the land unseen. Will their work live on? Will the institution hold faith with their ideals and beliefs? Will its doors remain open to the man of purpose to preach? Is this a selfish enterprise? These are some of the questions which must be answered.[6]

Ashley Johnson had contemplated the future of the college after his death. As early as 1912 he wrote the *Christian Stan-*

dard concerning the topic and identified four "considerations" that assured the continuation of the school: an ever-broadening support base ("steadfast friends"), more than adequate facilities and room for expansion, a strong faculty, and a noble purpose ("a preacher-training institution in a preacher-growing atmosphere").[7] As his health worsened he gave specific directions concerning the leadership of the college after his death. In October, 1922, the Johnsons legally transferred the property and control of Johnson Bible College to the trustees, effective upon the death of both of the founders. This will stipulated that Mrs. Johnson had the power to appoint her successor as president of the college and such successor must be a graduate of Johnson Bible College. Dr. Johnson charged the successor with responsibility of financial management of the college and that he should make an official annual report to the Board of Trustees. He declared that all of the Trustees must be members of the Church of Christ, and two-thirds of them must be graduates of Johnson Bible College. He gave the president the power to appoint his or her successor in office subject to the approval of the Board of Trustees.[8] In a subsequent "Last Will and Testament" in October, 1924, Dr. Johnson reaffirmed the original will and added more specific arrangements to provide for his wife and the college, which included the establishment of a trust fund to pay faculty salaries.[9] As a part of this trust fund agreement, Johnson required each president and faculty member to sign a document which affirmed that "he or she does believe the fundamental doctrines of the Christian Scriptures and has to the utmost of his or her ability endeavored to broadcast these principles among the students of Johnson Bible College."[10]

Emma Johnson was exercising her prerogative and, she believed, also fulfilling her husband's wishes by appointing Alva Ross Brown as President of Johnson Bible College one week before her death. Brown later confessed: "I am almost ashamed to admit that at that time I was only twenty-one."[11] The trustees attempted to dissuade him: he did not have the experience to operate a college; he had not earned the respect of the faculty and students; he was virtually unknown within the brotherhood of supporting churches. He was not experienced in ministry: could he train a young man to preach? He was not a poor southern boy: did he understand the value of hard work or the great need to educate laborers for the field? Did he have the evangelistic zeal of the founders? Was he committed to the industrial idea? Most of the trustees viewed his acceptance of the presidency as a prelude to disaster. Brown convinced the trustees, however, that whether they or anybody else thought he was capable, he was intent on following the instructions of Dr. and Mrs. Johnson, including acceptance of the position. In his view, the close connection with the Johnsons for the previous five years and "intimate knowledge of their plans and ideals" qualified him for the post. The Board of Trustees met on June 9, 1927, and approved Mrs. Johnson's appointment.

Two days later the Board sent a letter to the college constituency (which was also published in the *Christian Standard*) relating their actions. They announced the "satisfactory condition" of the faculty trust fund (thus ensuring the continuance of the college program) and the succession to the presidency of Alva Ross Brown and appealed for cooperation with their leadership. The letter acknowledged that at least one faculty member had left the college because of this decision but, in spite of this disappointment, the work would continue: "The administrative ideals will continue unchanged. We continue that spirit of the motto carved at one side of the entrance portal: Open day and night to the poor young man who desires above every other desire to preach the gospel of Christ."[12]

President Brown wrote a bold article in the *Standard* entitled, "Johnson Bible College Faces the Issue!" (subtitled, "Individuals pass on, but their works remain!"). He conveyed his deep commitment to the ideals of the founders and his perseverance in carrying on their work. After reference to Ashley Johnson's Last Will and Testament and his provisions to ensure the faithfulness of the college administration and faculty, Brown affirmed that he held these wishes as a "sacred trust." He acknowledged that there was opposition to his leadership and that he was disappointed in the way he and the college was being "misrepresented." He promised faithful adherence to the purpose of the college and announced an "urgent" need to raise ten thousand dollars to meet the pressing financial need. "Johnson Bible College is an open book," he concluded, and "any information concerning any feature of the work will be sent gladly." The article was accompanied by photographs and brief biographies of Professors William H. Sperry, Albert T. Fitts, and Henry R. Garrett.[13]

Brown did his best to convey to supporters and detractors alike his zeal for the ideals of Johnson Bible College. Approximately one year later he wrote in the *Blue and White* that the college must remain true to its fundamental principles: training men to preach the gospel, intense loyalty to the scriptures, preservation of its spiritual atmosphere; living by faith and prayer, and maintaining its "Open Door" to those without means who desired to preach. He enlisted the help of his faculty in his efforts to earn the respect of his detractors. Professor Garrett wrote an essay in the student paper, the *Johnson Junior* (the forerunner to the *Blue and White*), about the future of the college, in which he declared:

> Each worthwhile person . . . has his own objective to which all his thoughts, aspirations, and energies bend and which determines his value to the world. Likewise each valuable institution has its own great purpose, ideals, and standards: It [J.B.C.] is a preacher developing institution.[14]

In spite of these efforts, Brown faced several difficulties in his first years as president. Although enrollment was not diminished significantly, some students did not return to school in the fall after Mrs. Johnson's death. There was unrest among some faculty members and support from the alumni dwindled. Already faced with a "leftover" debt from the last few years of the Johnson administration, this lack of support was exacerbated by the shock of the stock market crash of October, 1929, and the subsequent economic depression.

The most constructive effort to resolve these problems was a Johnson Bible College luncheon and rally held at the International Convention in Washington, D.C., in October, 1930.[15] Over 125 supporters of the college gathered with the president and trustees at the Raleigh Hotel to develop a strategy for better relations between the college and its alumni. The Board of Trustees expressed intentions to play a more active role in the governing of the college and building better relationships with its supporters. The J.B.C. Alumni Association, which had disbanded in the final years of Dr. Johnson's presidency because of a lack of unified leadership, was reorganized and pledged to help raise twenty thousand dollars to relieve the college debt. The annual Homecoming, which had also been discontinued primarily because of the cost of travel, was announced for the following spring's commencement.

This was apparently a watershed meeting for the Brown administration. Even though the financial problems were not immediately alleviated and the Homecoming was not held, a more positive response from the alumni had resulted. President Brown wrote often in the *Blue and White* of the need for better cooperation, frankly acknowledging the difficulties he faced. He also often reaffirmed his commitment to the basic principles of the college: "it was my purpose to preserve the ideals of the past."[16] His tribute to the Johnsons, *Standing on the Promises*, was published in 1928 and convincingly demonstrated Brown's familiarity with those ideals. By the end of 1933 it seemed that he had weathered the storm of opposition and could now address the financial situation without distraction. The "boy-president" had been forced to mature quickly. J.B. Hunley reported his visit to the campus to the *Christian Standard* in December of that year and was impressed with what he witnessed:

> Many people thought that the death of President Johnson would mean the closing of the college. But, led by President Brown and an able faculty, and supported by the loyalty of a great student body and a wide circle of friends, the institution grows stronger each year. Ashley S. Johnson built more wisely than many of his contemporaries judged.[17]

The development of the college in the fourteen years of Brown's presidency was hindered greatly by a lack of funds. He not only confronted the Depression—and the college's base of support in the South and Midwest was hit especially hard—but also a brotherhood of churches in which financial support of agencies and institutions was a heated and divisive issue. The college lost a significant amount of its investment income, including some of its trust fund for faculty salaries, when the Fidelity Bankers Trust Company and S.W. Strauss and Company defaulted on a large percentage of their bonds and securities. The total college income for 1931-32 was $42,000; this was reduced to $23,000 in 1932-33. Expenditures for 1933-34 surpassed income by $6100.

No matter how frugal or adept at financial management Brown and his advisers might have been, the obstacles seemed insurmountable. He wanted to begin the administration building that Mrs. Johnson had initiated and even announced that the construction was underway. The project was scuttled a few months after the announcement, however, because of the onset of the Depression and the spiraling college debt. Brown, however, was able to report that between 1927 and 1933 nearly $29,000 worth of improvements were made to the physical plant of the college. This included a new faculty house and a summer kitchen in addition to needed repairs on the existing buildings.

One aspect of the college's financial principles was heartily retained by President Brown: the industrial department. His essay in the February 2, 1928 *Johnson Junior*, "Every Man a Man," reaffirmed Johnson's ideal of providing opportunity (work) for those without money for education. He called for "patience, responsibility," and "faithful attention to each one's task" on the part of the students and then added, "Ashley S. Johnson did all that he could to show that here is real merit in work that is honestly performed."[18] He made it clear to the *Christian Standard* in 1935 that the college would stand by its commitment to the "poor young man": "The institution pledges itself to help any man of proper qualifications who is eager to serve the Lord and willing to apply himself industriously."[19] Most of the work done by the students was on the farm and dairy, and their labors literally put food on their own table.

Enrollment at the college steadily increased after an initial decline, but still remained slightly less than the average enrollment under Dr. Johnson. From a low of 109 students in 1928, enrollment averaged 118 students through 1934 but then increased to an average of almost 140 for the last half of Brown's term (with a high of 152 in 1940). There were 155 graduates of the college under President Brown which, when compared to enrollment, reflects a graduation percentage of 8.5 percent. This is significant when compared to Ashley Johnson's 200 graduates (in 32 years) and graduation percentage of 5.1 percent. This increased graduation percentage also reflects the shift in the student body toward more college and less Academy students. Out of the 120 students enrolled in 1932 only 17 were in the Academy. These students continued to come from all parts of the United States and usually included foreign countries as well. For example, the 1937-38 student body represented twenty-nine states (almost equally divided between North, South, and West), four Canadian provinces, and two foreign countries (the Philippines and India).[20]

Alva Ross Brown was an accomplished scholar and educator and worked hard on improving the quality of education at Johnson Bible College. He made significant progress in raising the academic standards for both the faculty and the students. He was able to assemble a capable and stable faculty which included four professors—Helen Faye Stokes, Henry R. "Daddy" Garrett, Albert T. Fitts, and William O. Lappin—who remained with the college throughout Brown's entire term. The academic qualifications of the faculty were greatly improved under Brown, with nearly all of the professors holding a Masters degree and the rest having completed some graduate work. The use of student teachers was gradually phased out as the number of students in the Academy diminished. The contribution of the faculty during these years was marked by great personal sacrifice and dedication to the mission of the college. W. O. Lappin related that he went without salary from the college for several months at a time because of the financial distress.

President Brown improved the academic program for the students by creating a consistent curriculum designed specifically for the preaching ministry. Whereas he did not alter the basic educational philosophy or courses offered, he did arrange them in such a way to more effectively train the preacher.[21] The faculty understood how each department fit into this overall purpose. Professor of English Helen Stokes wrote in the *Blue and White*: "Why am I here? Because I want to place my life where it will count most for Him who has done so much for me. I can't preach myself, but I'm happy to have even a small share in preparing those who can."[22] The uniformity of the curriculum listed in the college catalogs from 1927-1940 (with only minor shifting and renaming of courses) indicates the stability of the academic program.

Approximately one-fifth of the courses were in Bible and several courses in math and science were retained. Reflecting concern about the influx of theological liberalism into the American seminaries in the 1920s, the catalogs from the Brown era contained an addendum to the Bible course listings:

> From the above it will be seen immediately that the Bible instruction given is thoroughly conservative. . . . The modern critical method is not used. . . . Destructive arguments are discussed and answered by the arguments of conservative scholars, men who believe thoroughly in the Deity of Jesus and in the inspiration of the Sacred Writing.[23]

Four years of languages were also required: two years each of Latin and Greek. A third year of Greek was offered for those who had previous language work in high school. The curriculum retained its liberal arts tendencies, with a central core of Bible courses.

One example of President Brown's concern for academics and their relationship to the church was a series of lectures delivered each Tuesday evening during the 1931-32 school year. This lectureship was sponsored by a local dentist, Dr. Carrick C. Cloud, and included prominent Christian businessmen, congressmen, judges, university professors, literary figures, educators, and preachers. The wide variety of topics (which included an address by a Knoxville rabbi on "Christ from a Jew's Point of View") reflected the breadth of Dr. Brown's interests and his concern that the preacher's education must also be built on a broad base.

Student life during the Brown years was characterized by both comedy and tragedy. A student string band, the "Kimberlin Kow-boys," performed often for the Alethian, Philodelphian, and Johnsonian Literary Societies. The "Silly Sallies," a society for the faculty and student wives, held regular receptions for the boys. Founder's Day was celebrated with the annual track meet, baseball game, and poetry contest. Miss Essie Bullock honored the birthdays each month with a supper and cake, and attempted to entice alumni to the annual Homecoming with the "impressive" promise that "we continue to serve Johnson-gravy, beans, biscuits, cornbread and sorghum."[24] Included in the notice that a tornado had hit the hen-house in March of

1930 and killed seventeen hens was the resulting fact that "consequently one hundred preachers practiced that branch of their pastoral functioning."[25] The Dixie Holstein Herd, of course, continued its blue ribbon ways and made the front page of the *Blue and White* on a couple of occasions. The death of "Old Toby," the delivery mule, was marked with congratulations "for 25-30 years of faithfully performing his duties."

Adversity was also a part of the Johnson experience during these years. A fire destroyed part of the Main Building in 1935. Unfortunate personal tragedies were also recorded. In the spring of 1934 Don Terwilliger drowned in the French Broad River. The calamity was repeated only one year later as two other students, John Sallee (age 19) and Clair Robison (age 26) also drowned in the river.[26]

The college also continued to enroll a small number of female students. A friendly debate continued over the "official" inclusion of female students. A student essay in the *Blue and White* affirmed the suggestion that J.B.C. should become a co-ed institution and offered "three points in favor": moral standards would not be lowered; women should be educated for the Lord's work, especially the mission field; and "preachers need educated wives."[27] Although there may have been a small increase in the number of female students in the college program during Brown's tenure, it was not significantly different from the number of females enrolled during the Johnson years. There were thirteen female students in 1936, nine in 1938, and eight in 1939. It appears that almost half of these were single women. A 1938 notice to the *Standard* listed four "unmarried girls" and five student wives "studying for Christian service."[28]

Despite the financial hardships which hampered travel, the students were involved in evangelism and service throughout the region. A survey of student activity for the month of February, 1940, reported that 28 students delivered 124 sermons to a total attendance of 7,538 people. These students had traveled 17,515 miles and preached in 43 different towns in 5 states. One student alone traveled 2500 miles, preached 25 sermons at 9 different places in Virginia, and reported "29 conversions and 20 baptisms."[29] Ruben Ratzlaff recorded the inspiring story of "Aunt Maggie," a blind black neighbor with whom many students visited, worked, sang, read the Scriptures, and prayed for many years.[30] The "Johnson Boys" established a mission in the Knoxville "slums" in 1940, holding services in the street and mills and organizing a Sunday School.

The students also did their part in support of the college. The Senior class of 1929 introduced the idea of a special Thanksgiving offering, requesting that each student send out ten letters asking for a monetary gift of one dollar to the college. The students presented an offering of $585 to President Brown on Thanksgiving of 1930. By 1938, the seniors set a goal of $1500 for the annual appeal. The senior class of 1940-41 led a drive to improve the Old Chapel by providing new stained glass windows, carpet, papering and varnishing. The students' loyalty and love for their Alma Mater was embodied in the words of the "Johnson Hymn," written by William Tucker in 1940. President Brown's final years were encouraging ones as the college graduated numerous talented and dedicated students who entered a variety of ministerial and educational fields.

Alva Ross Brown had suffered from a leaking heart valve for several years and the condition worsened through the winter of 1940-41. Weakened by influenza and possibly pneumonia, Brown died of heart failure on Sunday, March 2, 1941. His wife, Alma Childress Brown, and children, Robert Edward (Bobby) and Emma Elizabeth (Betty), sat with a host of friends in the college Chapel two days later and listened as trustee and former J.B.C. professor Robert M. Bell delivered the funeral tribute to President Brown. Dr. Bell praised Brown's "gifted" intellectual abilities, his "breadth and depth" of knowledge, his fine sense of humor, and his "renaissance" interests in art, music, the classics, and sports. Bell confessed his own skepticism of Brown's youth when he was appointed President: "Many of us thought he knew nothing much but books." He noted that Brown did not increase the size of the college but certainly improved its quality, citing the elevated educational standards. His greatest personal asset, according to Bell, was that "he had no selfish interests." Alva Ross Brown understood the essence of Johnson Bible College—in Dr. Bell's words, he had "caught the spirit of Ashley S. Johnson."[31]

After her husband's death Mrs. Alma Brown taught in the English departments at the University of Tennessee and Milligan College and, after "retirement," served as a high school librarian in the Knoxville City School system. Her excellent poetry has been published in *Summer Treasure and Other Poems* and more recently in *Hold Fast This Beauty* (1990). Her moving personification of the Main Building captured the "spirit" of Johnson Bible College and stands as a tribute not only to the college, but to the Browns' ministry and leadership:

THE MAIN BUILDING SPEAKS

I am the Main Building
Of Johnson Bible College.
I am more than brick and mortar—
More than stone and wood and glass.
I am a child of faith and hope.
I am the answer to a strong man's prayer.
Up from the blackness of despair,
And the bitterness of frustration,
From the cold ashes of my predecessor
In triumph I arose.

I have seen many seasons come and go.
I have seen the hills tenderly green in spring—
Crowned with the snowy lace of blossoming dogwood.
I have dreamed through long golden summer afternoons.
I have seen the maples clothed in scarlet dress
When the spell of Indian summer held the land.
I know the feel of lashing winter gales,
The sting of flying snow against my face.
Warm sunlight, slanting through
My stained glass windows,
Has caressed the cheeks of fair young brides,
Has bathed the rapt faces
Of men and women at morning worship,
And rested, oh, so lightly, on the brows
Of loved ones in death.

Sometimes at midnight,
When the many shadows creep,
And it is very still—
But for the swish and murmur of the river—
A strong presence seems to linger near,
And I find myself listening for a once familiar step.
But then I remember, and lean
A little more protectingly
Above the rugged granite marker
Glistening in the cold, white moonlight.

My corridors are deeply scarred
By the passing of many feet.
Throughout the years
I have remained steadfast in the purpose for which I was creat-
ed, and my doors
Are open day and night to poor young men—
As a mother hen covers her brood
So have I sheltered these.
I have heard them laugh and weep,
I have seen them work and play.
I am the very center of the life
Of Johnson Bible College.
I am the Main Building.

President Alva Ross Brown, 1936

President Alva Ross Brown, 1927

Alva Ross Brown,
JBC graduation picture, 1926

President Alva Ross Brown

Alva Ross Brown in front of Irwin Library

Alma and Alva Ross Brown on their wedding day, March 31, 1929

Mrs. Brown and children, Robert and Betty, c. 1940

President and Mrs. Brown beside the White House

President Brown, c. 1940

Mrs. Alma Childress Brown, Betty, and Robert at the presentation of the Brown presidential portrait, 1986.

Alma Brown as a public school librarian in Knoxville

Alma Brown viewing the Main Building plaque

Dean and Mrs. W.H. Sperry and children with President and Mrs. Ashley S. Johnson

Betty (Robison) Turner, Dean W.O. Lappin and Clair Robison, 1934

The JBC faculty and staff, c. 1928; (back) Johnson, Garrett, Fitts, Sperry; (center) McLarty, Brown, Lappin; (front) Stokes, Bullock

Professor and Mrs. Albert T. Fitts

Professor T.H. Johnson and family, 1927

Professor Henry R. "Daddy" Garrett

Professor Harold Hanlin as a JBC Senior, 1927

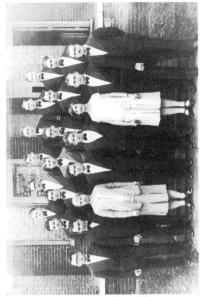

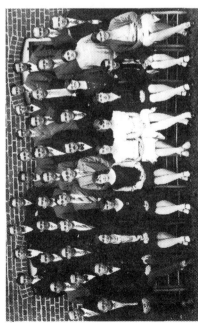

Upper Left: Alethian Literary Society, c. 1930; Upper Right: JBC Glee Club, Helen Stokes, director, 1929–30 Lower Left: JBC Orchestra, c. 1930; Lower Right: JBC students with Aunt Maggie, c. 1940

The Alethian Society's "Womanless Wedding," 1928

Edward Tesh, Ernest Galloway and Harold Enz missing their "girls," 1928

"Miss Essie" Bullock and her kitchen "boys," 1928

Delno Brown in his dormitory room, c. 1938

Frank Williams, driving, was employed for maintenance at the College at some time during tenure of all five presidencies. Allen Nance and Ed Tesh are on the bumper

Wilbur Reid and the JBC truck, c. 1933

Stage in the Original Gymnasium, 1920

Barry McLean bringing milk to the dining room, 1931

Men's basketball team, 1934–35

Basketball Game in the Old Gym (used from 1908 until 1951)

Women's basketball team, 1927–28

Alumni basketball team, 1933 Homecoming,

Chapter 4
An Inflamed Desire
1941–1968

In the summer of 1915, twenty-five year old Johnson Bible College student Robert Monroe Bell left the Hill at the end of his sophomore year and headed to Lannett, Alabama, to organize a revival meeting at the request of five men who wanted to start a church there. He obtained a tent for the meeting and asked Percy Cross to serve as the evangelist. The revival was immensely successful and the church was organized with 114 members. They immediately secured land and pledged three thousand dollars to erect a building. Bell was asked to stay and serve as minister with an offer of one thousand dollars plus room and board—a wonderful opportunity for this poor young man who desired so much to be a preacher. He was torn between continuing his education and launching his preaching career. Praying for guidance, Bell decided to accept President Ashley Johnson's advice as God's will. Dr. Johnson's reply was brief but to the point: "Come back even if they offer you five thousand." Robert Bell packed his bags and returned to Kimberlin Heights.[1] Neither Bell nor Johnson realized the magnitude of this decision.

The trustees of Johnson Bible College met early in 1941 to select Alva Ross Brown's successor as president of the college. Brown had served under difficult circumstances for fourteen years and his premature death at age thirty-five was certainly unexpected. No successor had been named by Brown, of course, and the choice would be crucial considering the status of the college. Despite heroic efforts by Brown to keep the college financially stable during the Depression, the institution was deeply in debt and on the verge of bankruptcy. The "favorite" choice for the presidency was S.S. Lappin, a renowned preacher, editor, educator, trustee of the college (appointed by Ashley Johnson himself), and brother of long-time J.B.C. professor W.O. Lappin. Lappin was promptly nominated by the trustees and it appeared that his accession to the presidency was assured.

Trustee Robert Bell (who was nominally offered the position before Lappin and had, as expected, respectfully declined), however, pointed out that Ashley Johnson's Last Will and Testament clearly specified that the president of Johnson Bible College must be a graduate of the institution. Since S.S. Lappin was not a graduate, his selection was improper. The trustees then offered the position to Harold Hanlin, a graduate of the college who was serving on the faculty of Butler School of Religion. After several days of deliberations, which included a visit to the campus, Hanlin declined. Several weeks passed with no success in finding a new president. Finally, the trustees settled on the one person who had tried so hard to find someone else: Robert M. Bell. He was elected at a called meeting of the trustees which was held in Cincinnati and assumed office on July 1, 1941.

Robert Monroe Bell was the perfect example of Ashley Johnson's poor southern boy in need of education to preach the gospel. He was born in Thomas County, Georgia, on June 15, 1889. Bell's mother died shortly after his birth and his father subsequently abandoned the family. Robert and his sister were left with their grandmother, Elizabeth Mims, who owned a 260 acre farm. From an early age Bell worked on the farm and at age twelve assumed its complete management. Grandmother Mims instilled the ethic of hard work and honesty into her grandson—along with a large dose of common sense about financial matters.

Robert faithfully attended the Methodist church with Mrs. Mims during these years. The family moved to a new farm near Spring Hill, Georgia, when he was fifteen and started attending the nearby Spring Hill Christian Church. He later reflected upon this life-changing decision:

> The first time I visited the Spring Hill Church, I did so out of pure curiosity. I wanted to see how the Campbellites acted. I

was disappointed at their perfectly normal and sane conduct. For various reasons, I returned again and again until I became a new creature in Christ.[2]

Confronted with the issue of immersion, Bell began a long and agonizing study of the Bible which included many heated discussions with the leaders of the Spring Hill church (and apparently any guest evangelist who came there to preach). Finally convinced of the New Testament teaching concerning baptism and convicted of the need for a church that preached the New Testament message without denominational controversies, Bell obeyed the Gospel and was baptized in 1908 at age nineteen. He immediately began plans to enter the ministry.

Because of his responsibilities with the farm, Robert only completed the fourth grade in school. When he was eighteen, he recognized the need to continue his formal education. Bell returned to the Spring Hill Grade School and finished grades five through eight in six months. He applied to Transylvania University but was rejected because of his lack of education and money. In the summer of 1910 a Johnson Bible College student came to hold a revival meeting at Spring Hill and told Bell of the opportunity to work while he obtained an education. Bell discussed this with his grandmother (who was overjoyed with her grandson's decision to become a preacher) and with her approval sold one bale of cotton—for seventy-one dollars, his year's wages—and enrolled at Johnson Bible College.

Bell finished eighth grade grammar and arithmetic and the entire high school course in three years. He entered the college department and quickly became a "favorite son" of Ashley Johnson. Maintaining the work ethic learned as a youth, Bell worked as a bookseller and professional photographer in addition to his twenty-five and one-half hours on the college work program. After his sophomore year, Dr. Johnson suggested that he go to Lannett even though he had "no experience, no plans, and only three hastily prepared sermons."[3] After a series of cottage prayer meetings, debate with a Methodist minister, and tent-meeting revival, the church was established.

Accepting Dr. Johnson's advice, Bell returned to J.B.C. in the fall of 1915 to complete another year. The next summer, again at Dr. Johnson's suggestion, he went to Canada with two

other students under the auspices of the Provisional Missionary Society. Repeating the success he had enjoyed in Alabama,
Bell decided to remain with the congregation he helped establish in St. James, a suburb of Winnipeg. He attended the University of Manitoba, studying economics and history. After one
year, Bell returned to Johnson as a senior and graduated with
the class of 1918.

Upon graduation Bell applied for a chaplaincy position with
the United States Navy. His military career, however, lasted
only three months: World War I ended on November 11. Bell
returned to Canada as a missionary under the Christian Wom-
en's Board of Missions. In addition to a successful ministry, he
began work with the Canadian Brotherhood Federation, an organization which raised money for war relief in Europe among
various churches. He resigned from his preaching ministry and
became Provincial Secretary for the Federation. Bell quickly
became dissatisfied with this position, however, and wrote Dr.
Johnson for help in finding another suitable preaching ministry. He told Johnson of his forthcoming marriage and urged
him to send a reply to his fiancee's home in Jacksonville, Flori-
da.

Robert Bell married Myrtle Dekle in Jacksonville on June
15, 1920. They soon received a surprising invitation from President Johnson to return to the college to teach. The Bells arrived in August, 1920, and Robert began his duties as
professor of English, literature, economics, and history. In the
summer of 1923 he enrolled at the University of Tennessee and
subsequently completed a Master of Arts degree in Economics
(1927). While pursuing his degree, Bell was offered a position
in the School of Business Administration to teach economics at
the university. Bell wrote Dr. Johnson, who was in Chicago at
the time undergoing medical treatment, and expressed the desire to accept the position. He soon received Johnson's reply
which carried the heading, "Oh, my son Absalom!" and voiced
disapproval and feelings of betrayal.[4] Bell nevertheless accepted the university's offer and began teaching economics in the
fall of 1924. The once-intimate, warm relationship he had enjoyed with the Johnsons was never completely restored.

Bell was a professor of economics at the University of Tennessee for seventeen years, teaching transportation and traffic

management in addition to his economics courses. Shortly before his accession to the presidency of Johnson Bible College, Bell was offered the position of Head of the Department of Economics at the University of Tennessee, Martin—which he declined in favor of remaining in Knoxville where he enjoyed a prominent position as a university professor and community leader.

He was also employed by the American Institute of Banking and taught night courses in Money and Banking, Banking Economics, and Analysis of Financial Statements. This "night school" was later augmented by courses sponsored by the Retail Credit Association, the Wholesale Credit Association of Knoxville, and the Independent Merchant Association. Bell once estimated that "fifty percent of the bank officers in Knoxville had been students in his classes at one time or another."[5] During his tenure at the university Bell also benefited from valuable experience in the real estate and investment business.

While he was making the initial transition from the Bible college to the university, Bell accepted a request to "fill in" preach at the First Christian Church in Harriman, Tennessee, whose minister had recently resigned. The "filling in" lasted twenty-one years. During this time Bell maintained close contact with Johnson Bible College. He was a friend and strong supporter of President Brown and began service as a trustee of the college in 1938. In recognition of his service to the college and the brotherhood, Bell was awarded honorary doctorates from both Milligan College and Johnson Bible College.

Dr. and Mrs. Bell had two children, Bobby and Betty. In the fall of 1940, Bobby, a nineteen year old sophomore at the University of Tennessee, was killed in an automobile accident. One result of this tragedy in Dr. Bell's life was a reawakening of his appreciation for Ashley Johnson. Dr. Johnson had once confessed to Bell: "When my baby died, Johnson Bible College was born. I was soon to have more sons than I could have ever had myself."[6] Dr. Bell's feeling of "kinship" with Johnson fueled a new commitment to the work of the college—and became a major turning point in his life and in the history of Johnson Bible College.

Dr. Bell faced several difficulties in the first years of his presidency, including a college debt of over fifty thousand dollars, division within the Restoration Movement which not only affected the financial support base of the college but also called for the college to "take sides" in theological controversies, and controversy over the limitation on the president's salary dictated by Dr. Johnson's will. In his usual way, Dr. Bell took steps to face and resolve these issues. For example, he wrote his "Statement of Aims for J.B.C." in the June 20, 1942 edition of the *Blue and White*:

> When I accepted the presidency of Johnson Bible College, I did so with the definite understanding that the College belongs to the Church and is a servant of the Church. With these facts in mind, I set about my new duties in the hope of accomplishing the following definite objectives.
>
> 1. To pay off, as quickly as possible, the floating debt and to put the college on a cash basis. . .
>
> 2. . . . to put the buildings and equipment in a good state of repair. . .
>
> 3. . . . to develop the strongest Faculty that can be assembled with what we have to offer . . .
>
> 4. . . . to employ a good evangelist as a regular member of our Faculty.

Robert Bell had been connected with Johnson Bible College for thirty-one years as student, professor, and trustee and clearly understood his task. The development of the college during his presidential term may be understood by an examination of how these objectives were achieved under his leadership.

When Dr. Bell assumed the presidency the college owed more than fifty thousand dollars to its creditors. Twelve thousand dollars of this amount were past-due accounts and many of the creditors assumed they would never be paid. The endowment fund established to pay faculty salaries had been virtually depleted (at least thirty-two thousand dollars had been "borrowed" to pay operating expenses) and faculty salaries had not been fully paid since 1933. In addition to the debt, the college buildings were in a bad state of disrepair:

> Roofs are leaking, termites are eating up foundations, the water tank and heating plant are in bad condition, and much of the farm machinery is worn out. To make these repairs will require

a minimum of $4,500. This does not include repairs for the frame dormitory.[7]

While serving as trustee, Bell had led an effort to relieve this debt but only served to postpone the inevitable financial malady. Acting President W.O. Lappin conducted an emergency appeal for funds in the summer of 1941 and raised $11,700 in 75 days. This amount enabled Lappin to alleviate the faculty salary deficit. It did not solve the debt problem. Dr. Bell later reflected on his first few months as President and the pressing financial problems:

> When I accepted the Presidency . . . I firmly resolved that "whatever happens, I will not worry." But within a week my resolution was badly bent. Within a month it was battered and broken. The trouble? Debts. Bills! Bills!! Bills!!! and no money to pay them.[8]

President Bell immediately sent letters to the supporters of the college, explaining the financial situation and appealing for funds. Enough gifts were received from this appeal to reduce the past-due accounts debt to $5,000 in September and completely erase this amount by the end of the year.[9]

Dr. Bell's plan to alleviate the college debt included the development of a wider base of support from the friends and alumni of the college. The J.B.C. Alumni Association had functioned sporadically during Dr. Brown's presidency and much of its vital contribution had been lost to the college. The Association was reorganized at the 1942 North American Christian Convention in Indianapolis under the leadership of F. Burton Doyle and played an increasingly important role in the development of the institution. The Alumni Association was instrumental in improving communication among its members, supporting churches, and potential students. The annual Homecoming and Preaching Rally (moved from commencement to February in 1957) sponsored by the Alumni Association was re-established and developed from a small gathering during most of the Bell years into the foremost event of the current college calendar. The first major project sponsored and completed by the alumni was the construction of the Memorial Chapel in 1960-61. This project laid an important foundation for increased alumni participation in the life of the college.

Along with the improvement of alumni involvement came a desire to give the alumni a more responsible role in the leadership of the college. In 1963 the Council of Seventy was established. This body of alumni was elected by the Association to serve in an advisory capacity to the trustees and "to promote the general welfare of the College." Glen Wheeler served as its first president. This broad base of leadership and improved relationships with the churches they represented enabled President Bell and his administration to focus more intently upon the task of educating preachers of the gospel.

Dr. Bell's second goal was to improve the physical plant. In addition to general repair of the existing buildings, many improvements and additions were completed. New professor's homes were added, dormitories renovated and expanded, offices remodeled, and shop areas enlarged. Five major construction projects were completed under the Bell administration: the Gymnasium (dedicated in 1951), Girl's Dormitory (Myrtle Hall, 1951), Married Couple's Dormitory (Bell Hall, 1955), Chapel (Alumni Memorial, 1962), and Library and Administration building (Glass Memorial Library, 1965). The construction of the earlier buildings was personally overseen by Dr. Bell who often served as financier, architect, and construction engineer. Faculty members such as Floyd E. Clark provided much of the construction supervision and the students much of the labor through the college work program.

President Bell was committed to Ashley Johnson's "industrial ideal." He had come to J.B.C. without means to pay for his education, worked hard in the Industrial Department, and greatly appreciated the opportunity offered through this system. He sympathized with the struggling students and remained firm in his intention to continue the work program, even though it had become a financial burden on the college. In spite of this fact—which Dr. Bell was well aware of—the work program remained a central feature of the institution. Bell's affirmation of the program sounded the theme so familiar from the Johnson years: "It is possible for a student to get an education at Johnson Bible College even if he has no money at all. But he must have character, energy, and purpose."[10] He summarized his conviction about the "Self-Help Department" in the college catalogs:

At the present time perhaps more men are financially able to go through college than thirty or forty years ago. But there are still many with the talents and earnestness to succeed who are hindered by lack of funds; there are still poor boys who desire to preach. Consequently, the college has retained its industrial feature.[11]

In addition to the work program, the college benefited from an increasing number of scholarships and giving plans for financial aid developed by the Bell administration. By the mid-1960s the character of work-study was significantly altered by the wide availability of government-sponsored scholarships, grants, and loans. Operation of the farm was greatly reduced— again, government health and agriculture regulations partially influenced this decision—which removed a source of productive work to offer the students.

President Bell's third objective at the beginning of his term was to develop the strongest faculty possible. During the early years of his presidency he did experience conflict with some of the faculty joined with student dissatifaction that was expressed to the alumni and larger Johnson constituency, but he overcame these difficulties by patience, a nonvindictive spirit, and persistent attention to the work at hand. Age and personal circumstances also contributed to faculty attrition during those early years. Albert Fitts had retired shortly before President Brown's death. Professor Helen Stokes, another key faculty member, left the faculty in 1942 to marry Frank Kerns and subsequently taught at Dallas Christian College. Two of the most beloved faculty members who served the college for a combined total of fifty-two years retired during Bell's presidency. Henry R. "Daddy" Garrett retired in 1947 at age eighty-one. Professor Garrett taught at Milligan College for seventeen years and Lincoln Memorial University for five years in addition to a successful preaching career in churches in Tennessee, Texas, and Georgia. He was President of Stuart Normal College (1894-95), Milligan College (1903-08), and Midland College (1911-13). He came to J.B.C. in 1926 and taught Bible, Mathematics, Sociology, and Economics. Several tributes written to Professor Garrett shared one common theme: "Probably no teacher was ever more universally loved by his students." Garrett was awarded the degree of Doctor of Literature by

Johnson Bible College in 1936. "Daddy" Garrett was buried in the small cemetery in the field near the front gate of the college.

"Dean" William Otis Lappin remained on the faculty for a significant portion of Bell's term, retiring in 1959 after thirty-one years of service to the college. After completing college work at the University of Chicago, Dean Lappin began preaching at Saybrook, Illinois, in 1898. His fifteen years of ministry in several Illinois churches was followed by a forty-six year teaching career. W.O. Lappin taught at Atlantic Christian College (Wilson, North Carolina), Morehead Normal School, Kentucky (where he also served as President), and Milligan College prior to his thirty-one years at Johnson. He taught History, Philosophy, and Bible and was especially remembered for his careful scrutiny of student behavior in his classes and in the dormitory—a summons to Dean Lappin's office was a fearful thing! He served as Acting President of J.B.C. following the death of President Brown in March, 1941 until the accession of Dr. Bell in October of that year. Dean Lappin was honored by the college for his 61 years of service as minister of the Gospel, teacher, and administrator in May, 1959, by receiving an honorary Doctor of Laws degree.

Dr. Bell was faced with the task of assembling a practically new faculty. He clearly outlined the criteria for selecting faculty members for the college. Four questions were asked of each candidate: "1. What does he believe? 2. Does he know the subjects which he will be required to teach? 3. Can he teach? 4. Can he stimulate and inspire his students?"[12] President Bell required each faculty member to affirm the doctrinal statement drafted by Dr. Johnson. He stated that he "has no patience with those teachers who can 'teach it either way' or have one theology for the classroom and another for the pulpit."[13] He sought to increase the academic qualifications of the faculty (by the end of his term two faculty members had earned doctorates). Two members, Floyd E. Clark and Robert E. Black, would be recognized by the college for faithful long-term distinguished service with honorary doctorates. Three members served the college for twenty-five years or more: Dr. Lovella Richardson (1958-1985) and Professors Clark and Ruth Rowland (1950-75). Three currently serve on the faculty at J.B.C.:

Lee Richardson (since 1957), J. O. Pierson (since 1960), and Joel F. Rood (since 1965). The current administration of the college includes faculty members who were recruited by and served under Dr. Bell: President David L. Eubanks (1958), Academic Dean William R. Blevins (1963), and Dean of Students John M. Lowe (1966).

The academic program of the college, which was strengthened throughout President Brown's term, saw further positive development under Dr. Bell. The Academy was disbanded in 1941 because most enrolling students had opportunity to attend high school. The college did arrange a limited number of high school level classes for those with academic deficiencies. The basic Bachelor of Arts ministerial degree remained the standard program throughout the Bell years. Degrees such as the Bachelor of Sacred Literature (initiated in the mid-1940s primarily for female students), Bachelor of Sacred Music (introduced 1953-54), and an education and secretarial minor for the B.S.L. were added. A Master of Theology degree with a major in New Testament and minor in Church History was offered from 1956-59 and required an additional thirty semester hours plus a thesis. This degree evolved into the Bachelor of Theology, a five-year undergraduate course of study.

An analysis of the curriculum for the Bachelor of Arts degree from 1941-1967 reveals very little change in the overall program or educational philosophy of the college. The curriculum averaged approximately one-third of the work taken in biblical studies, one-third in general studies, and one-third in professional-theological studies. Significant changes in the curriculum included the reduction of the Greek language requirement from three to two years, the removal of mathematics courses after 1945-46, and the decrease of church history courses after 1958-59.

The one single important influence on the development of the curriculum was the official admittance of female students in 1948. The catalog of the following year announced:

Due to the increasing demand for religious education directors and competent pastors' assistants, a limited number of women students have been admitted to Johnson Bible College. During the 1948-49 year, about one-fifth of the students were women. While this represents a somewhat higher proportion than in years before, there have always been some women in training at J.B.C. These women have been admitted on essentially the same terms as men: a commitment to full-time Christian service in some capacity.[15]

This notice was reprinted in the September 1952 edition of the *Blue and White* with an added remark:

Facilities at Johnson Bible College will not permit acceptance of a large number of women students, but those who can prove themselves to be worthy and who apply early enough in advance, will be accepted so far as these facilities permit.[16]

The addition of female students required course offerings other than the Bachelor of Arts (Ministerial). Even though opportunities for professional positions for music, youth, and Christian education directors, church secretaries, and missionaries were available to women, the churches that formed the supportive constituency for Johnson Bible College did not ordain women to the preaching ministry. Programs such as the Bachelor of Sacred Literature and Bachelor of Sacred Music were developed, therefore, with specializations in education, secretarial work, and church music.

Enrollment of female students steadily increased during the Bell era as the following table suggests:

YEAR	TOTAL ENROLLMENT	MALE	FEMALE
1941	136	128	8
1945	97	67	30
1949	159	122	37
1953	169	110	59
1959	184	115	69
1962	210	121	89
1967	236	148	88

The percentage of women in the total student body increased from twenty-five percent in 1948 to thirty-seven percent in 1968. The construction of Myrtle Hall in 1951 as a dormitory for female students has already been noted.

Although Dr. Bell attempted to make it clear that female students must be committed to full-time Christian service and their inclusion would not alter the primary purpose of the college, their presence created some alteration in the official purpose statement. The 1964-65 college catalog changed "young men" to "young people," and "preach the gospel" to "preach and teach the gospel."[17] The admittance of females was seen by most observers of the college as a positive step forward in its development, but it created a dilemma for a college that was started for the "poor young man" and whose primary purpose was to educate students for a vocation—the preaching ministry—which traditionally excluded women.

Another issue that emerged during the Bell era in relationship to the academic program was accreditation. Ashley Johnson opposed standardization on the grounds that the college was a special purpose institution and accreditation would require it to diminish its distinct emphasis on preaching and evangelism. This attitude toward accrediting associations was continued well into the presidency of Dr. Bell. In his discussion of the historical development of this policy, Robert Black commented that "secular college associations which set up the standards determining membership in the associations make no provision for colleges operated on faith in God . . . ."[18] He also quoted Alva Ross Brown's 1938 statement that the college's academic program was arranged "without any inclination to follow the arbitrary standard of secular college associations."[19]

Financial circumstances concerning student aid from federal and state government support of education fostered a re-examination of this attitude by the early 1950s. In 1951 Dr. Bell applied for accreditation from the Accrediting Association of Bible Institutes and Bible Colleges (AABC). He explained his motivation in the October, 1952 *Blue and White*:

> During the first fifty-seven years of its operation JBC never applied to any accrediting agency for accreditation of its work. The founder . . . was an individualist who preferred to do his work in his own way without interference from outsiders. His objective was to train preachers to preach the Gospel as it is written; and he felt sure that he could accomplish that objective just as well without the approval of an accrediting association as he could with it. His successors, President Brown and myself, assumed the same attitude.
>
> In recent years, however, two situations have developed to make accreditation necessary. . . . the Federal government, through its various G.I. bills, is entering more and more into the field of education. Because of the belief that many schools have

sprung up primarily to get payments from the government and
from veterans, non-accredited schools are being looked upon
with disfavor by governmental agencies. Accreditation removes
that disfavor and will simplify the problem of veterans who
wish to enroll in Johnson Bible College under the new law.

[Secondly] . . . competition between and among colleges for
students is becoming increasingly keen. . . . In recent years several prospective students, who had already sent applications to
Johnson, were told that credits earned at Johnson would be no
good, because Johnson was not an accredited school. The students, not knowing the significance of accreditation, were easily
persuaded to go elsewhere.[20]

Johnson Bible College received full and unconditional accreditation from the AABC on October 16, 1952. Anticipating
opposition from college supporters, Dr. Bell pointed out that

Such accreditation does not make our work any better. It is
merely recognition by an accrediting association that the work
done at JBC is of standard quality . . .

It was not . . . for the benefit of deans and professors of graduate schools that we sought accreditation. They already knew of
the excellency of our work. Nor was it for the benefit of the
churches who employ our graduates. . . . We sought accreditation for the benefit of the poor prospective Freshman who was
being told, falsely, that credits earned at Johnson were no good
because the school was not accredited.[21]

Three years later, however, J.B.C. withdrew from the Accrediting Association. The accreditation committee determined
that the Board of Trustees needed more professional businessmen and asked Dr. Bell to have Ashley Johnson's will changed
to accommodate this arrangement. They also had objections to
the virtually unlimited power of the president over the institution—especially his appointment of trustees. By 1965 Dr. Bell
applied for re-instatement, but it was not obtained during his
administration. In fact, this experience with the Association
induced some alumni, faculty, and administration members to
further question the validity of accreditation.

The fourth objective in President Bell's original agenda for
the college was to increase the college's contribution to the
evangelization of the world. Bell had learned well at the feet of
Ashley Johnson and had a great zeal for evangelism and concern for church growth. This spirit was clearly captured in a

brief essay entitled "Why I Entered the Ministry" written early
in Dr. Bell's presidency. After acknowledging an early prejudice
against preachers learned from his family (his favorite uncle
called them "beggars, chicken eaters, loafers and ladies' men")
and describing his initial attraction to the "Campbellites," Bell
explained why he chose to preach:

> I came to feel that division among believers as expressed in de-
> nominationalism was of the devil, and that the restoration of
> the New Testament church was the most important task to
> which any man could devote his life. That is why at the age of
> twenty-one, with only a grammar-school education, I entered
> Johnson Academy with the hope of becoming a preacher. That is
> why during my eighteen years on the faculty of the University
> of Tennessee I drove 100 miles every Sunday to preach. That is
> why I left the university two years ago and came back to John-
> son Bible College to train preachers.
>   I still believe that the gospel is the power of God unto salva-
> tion and that the restoration of the New Testament church is
> the most important task to which any man can devote his life.[22]

President Bell was deeply committed to the original purpose of
the college: "to train faithful men to preach the gospel." He declared at the Jubilee celebration that college would not be di-
verted from its work as a preacher-training institution: "All of
its resources have been and will continue to be devoted to that
one purpose. At J.B.C. training preachers is not a side line.
This one thing we do."[23] He later affirmed that under his leadership the college would never "break faith with this
tradition."[24]

In addition to the training of ministers through the college
program, Dr. Bell encouraged evangelistic efforts throughout
the churches. A letter offering a one hundred dollar "J.B.C.
Evangelism Award" to the most effective evangelistic campaign
was sent to over four thousand preachers and churches. The
Blue and White traced the development of this "contest," an-
nouncing the winning church (Central Christian of Covington,
Tennessee) and detailing the various ideas and programs that
were submitted. A Christian service camp was established on
campus for young people in the summer of 1946 which especially emphasized commitment to full-time Christian service
(the camp was moved in 1975 to Smoky Mountain Christian

Camp in Coker Creek, Tennessee). Most members of the college faculty preached in Knoxville-area churches in addition to
holding numerous revivals, leadership clinics, and missions
rallies. The Smoky Mountain Men's Fellowship was formed
with much influence from the college and was instrumental in
establishing numerous churches in the Knoxville and Chattanooga area. Dr. Bell took seriously the principle that the college was the servant of the church.

Under Dr. Bell's editorship, the *Blue and White* became an
influential publication within the churches of the Restoration
Movement. He recommended that ministers use the paper to
"carry the gospel to those who do not attend church, . . . the
message of the Restoration Movement to the denominational-
ists, and . . . the importance of New Testament evangelism to
our own brethren."[25] President Bell increasingly used the *Blue
and White* as an organ to communicate his views on important
doctrines and issues. He addressed fundamental doctrines of
the Christian faith, principles of New Testament Christianity,
controversy within the churches of Christ over instrumental
music, and the divisiveness of denominationalism. He carried
on a lively correspondence with both proponents and oppo-
nents of his views through its pages. Dr. Bell once wrote to a
friend that his favorite sport was writing editorials for the *Blue
and White!*[26]

When Dr. Bell became president, the college was caught in
the middle of the division between the Disciples and Independents over theological liberalism (especially in institutions of
higher learning) and organization of church-related agencies.
He was president during most of the "Decade of Decision," the
1960s, in which the Disciples of Christ wing of the movement
voted in favor of Restructure and formed a denominational organization. The heated debate and tragic strife that characterized these events affected Johnson students, alumni, faculty,
and supporting churches and individuals. Bell was often asked,
"Where Does Johnson Stand?" and he attempted to steer a
careful course. He condemned open membership and the "denominational" nature of agencies and strongly opposed Restructure, clearly aligning himself and the college with the
conservatives. He criticized, however, the divisiveness of many
within the Independent group (for example, an essay in the

Blue and White entitled "The Independents Who are Splitting the Brotherhood"), served on the Commission to Restudy the Disciples of Christ (a body which advocated unity within the movement), and addressed both the North American Christian Convention and the International Convention. He declared that "Johnson Bible College has refused to become sectarianized or denominationalized."[27] In response to the criticism that J.B.C. no longer educated ministers for the Disciples of Christ churches, Bell wrote:

> If your church is still an undenominational Christian Church, interested in spreading the unadulterated Gospel of Christ, pleading for the unity of all disciples upon faith in Christ and obedience to Him rather than upon the support of a particular agency, then your church and I are still working for the same great cause. On the other hand, if you and your church have accepted a denominational status and are interested only in unifying disciples upon their support of a certain agency or group of agencies, then it is you who have changed, and it is I who am disappointed.[28]

Although Dr. Bell was firm in his convictions and clearly stated the college's stance without compromise, he was able to guard the college from an inordinate amount of controversy. His idea was to remain nonsectarian—unaligned with any particular group—and serve the entire brotherhood of churches. The circumstances generated by the official adoption of Restructure in 1969, creating the Christian Church (Disciples of Christ), however, made it difficult to fulfill his dream that the college serve all churches within the Restoration heritage.

A discussion of the Bell era would be incomplete without mention of the contribution of Mrs. Bell. When alumni from this period are asked about life on the campus when they were students, nearly all mention working for Mrs. Bell. She was a determined gardener, desperate to bring beauty to the "Wilderness," as she called the area below the president's home. She was also a gracious hostess who transformed many uncouth young students into accomplished waiters and opened the doors of the White House to innumerable guests. Mrs. Bell died on January 3, 1988. Floyd Clark summarized her contribution at the 1971 Homecoming tribute to her life and ministry:

So far as our life here is concerned, the second most fateful decision that was made by our guest this afternoon was following the death of her son. She decided that she could adopt the boys on the Hill and somehow compensate for her grief and loss and she transferred the love she had given Bobby to the men on the Hill. . . .

Since those days, she has given to her boys a mother's love and affection. She has scolded them, she has worked them, she has spoiled them. . . . More than five thousand students whose lives have been touched by our guest will be forever in her debt for she fought and cried like a tigress for her boys. . . . Boys who once waited tables and served her guests with honor and distinction now serve the Lord with honor throughout this nation and overseas.[29]

By fall, 1967, Johnson Bible College was in the best condition in its history. Financial stability, strong alumni support, an adequate and well-maintained physical plant, and a well-trained and experienced faculty greeted the largest class (236) ever enrolled in the history of the school. Few would have suggested that this twenty-seventh year of the presidency of Robert M. Bell would be his last. Dr. Bell suffered a heart attack on February 9, 1968, and was still in the hospital when the alumni and students gathered for Homecoming the following week. The Thursday (February 15) afternoon preaching session was drawing to a close when his daughter, Betty Bell Barker, came to the platform and announced that her father had died at 1:00 that afternoon. She spoke only a few moments to the assembly, expressing her and her father's confidence in the alumni, respect for the Board of Trustees, and love for Johnson Bible College. Her thoughts—like many others present at that gathering—were on the future of the college. As she was giving advice on how to treat the next president of the college, Betty spoke these words:

It is the end of an era. It was a marvelous era and I'm glad to have been a part of it. But it's over and my father can't run Johnson Bible College from the grave.

. . . I think the Lord felt that it was time for a change, and we have to accept the Lord's will, don't we?[30]

R.M. Bell — JBC graduation picture, 1918

Robert M. Bell as University of
Tennessee Professor, c. 1930

President Bell, c. 1941

President Bell, c. 1965

Chaplain R.M. Bell, 1918

The Aletheian Debating Team,
1914–15: Andy Anderson, R.M.
Bell, Clayton Wilson

R.M. Bell working as a photographer

Dr. Johnson promised Bob Bell a
full page in the 1914–15 catalog if
he let his beard grow all summer.

Mrs. Myrtle Dekle Bell   Mrs. Bell in the White House, 1943

Dr. and Mrs. Bell, c. 1960   Mrs. Bell telling Mayo Proctor
                                where to plant the flowers during a
                                visit to campus, 1978

R.M. Bell in his room as a student at the University of Manitoba, 1916–17

Professor and Mrs. R.M. Bell with President and Mrs. Ashley Johnson, c. 1920

R.M. Bell, Minister at First Christian Church, Harriman, Tennessee, c. 1940

President Bell in the White House, c. 1955

President Bell and the Alumni Chapel Committee, c. 1960

President Bell and secretary Gertie Kostik, c. 1965

President Bell at the dedication of the Married Couples Dormitory (later named Bell Hall), 1955

President Bell and the Dixie Holstein Herd, 1943

Glass Memorial Library, dedicated 1965

The gymnasium/swimming pool, dedicated 1951

Women's dormitory (later named Myrtle Hall), dedicated 1951

President Bell (far right) "inspecting" construction on Married Couples Dormitory, 1954

The White House, c. 1950

The dairy barn and the "mule barn," c. 1950

**Alumni Memorial Chapel,
dedicated, 1962**

**Alumni Chapel Committee
Chairman Glen Wheeler
at the dedication**

1965 Commencement in Alumni Memorial Chapel

President Bell and JBC Faculty, 1951: Mr. and Mrs. Rowland, Holland, Clark, Bell, Lappin, Black, and Bligh

JBC Faculty, 1963: Rowland, Richardson, Clark, Bell, Pierson, (front) Eubanks, Rowland, Richardson, Simkins, and Black

Professor Robert E. Black teaching Old Testament, c. 1955

P.H. Welshimer, Trustee
1938–1958

Oren E. Long, JBC Alumnus/profes-
sor, later territorial governor and first
U.S. senator from Hawaii

S. S. Lappin, Trustee, 1926–61
W.O. Lappin, Professor, 1928–59

Dr. and Mrs. Floyd Clark and daughter Betty Ann at the dedication of
the Alumni Chapel — 1962

Gertie Kostik,
President's secretary, 1947–72

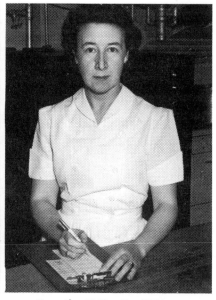

Dorothy "Miss Dot" West,
Dietician, 1951–56

Helen Campbell Bourne, Secretary
and Trustee under Ashley Johnson;
Housemother and English Professor
under Dr. Bell

Jean Morgan, Dietician, 1960–88

JBC Choir with Mrs. Lorraine Brown, Director, 1947

Class of 1955 in front of Bell Hall (still under construction)

Students in the classroom of the Main Building

The JBC library staff, 1950

JBC Choir, Clark Rowland, Director, c. 1953

Stage and cast of "The Everlasting Arms," a drama written and directed by Floyd E. Clark

JBC students involved in street ministry in downtown Knoxville, 1946

Dr. and Mrs. Floyd Clark in front of tent used for the 1966 summer tour of "The Everlasting Arms"

The JBC Choir bus, 1951

Oren E. Long (left) was appointed Governor of the Territory of Hawaii by President Harry Truman. When that territory became a state Governor Long became its first U.S. senator. Senator Long had been Secretary of State of the territory and before that served for many years as Superintendent of Public Education. He graduated from JBC in 1911 and taught and was principal of the JBC academy from 1914-17. The college presented him with the Doctor of Laws degree following his address to the graduating class of 1960.

Thornton Charles Miller (right) was a student at JBC 1909-14. As a navy chaplain he rendered notable service following the disaster at Pearl Harbor December 7, 1941, being in full charge of burying the dead and taking care of the dependent families. He was promoted to the rank of Rear Admiral in 1947, became the Senior Chaplain in the three services (Army, Navy, and Air Corps) and was appointed Chaplain Corps Inspector. At the request of General MacArthur's staff he flew to Tokyo to deliver the Easter sermon to the armed forces of the Pacific in 1951. JBC awarded Chaplain Miller the Doctor of Laws degree following his address at commencement, 1950.

Softball team, 1956–57

Basketball game in the gymnasium, c. 1955

"Coach" Bill Blevins and his intramural basketball team, 1957

Tug-of-war over the pond, 1942

Aerial view of JBC campus, 1968

Presidential Cemetery, 1968

Board of Trustees convened after the death of President Bell, 1968: Scott, McKowen, Jones, Clarke (Chairman), Reid, Phillips, and Wheeler

Dr. Floyd E. Clark, Acting Executive Vice-President, 1968–69

Floyd and Billie Clark with Mrs. R.M. Bell

Dr. and Mrs. Floyd Clark with President Eubanks and Academic Dean Blevins

The "Doctors": Floyd Clark, Berton Clarke, Wilbur Reid, Sr., receiving honorary degrees from President Eubanks, 1969

Chapter 5
A Steadfast Desire
1968–1992

On a Sunday evening in August, 1989, Johnson Bible College President David L. Eubanks arrived at the Bearden Christian Church in west Knoxville to discuss the college's Centennial Campaign with the congregation. It was the same church to which Ashley Johnson had appealed for a word of encouragement to continue forward with his plan to establish the school nearly one hundred years earlier. A member of the Bearden church, Brother Crippen, promised to give one hundred dollars to Dr. Johnson—the first contribution to Johnson Bible College. President Eubanks walked past the same pulpit from which Ashley Johnson spoke (now on display in the vestibule of the church building) and greeted the thirty or forty members of the church who had assembled for the evening. Half of the group were Johnson students. Many of the remainder were widows. There were certainly larger, more prosperous churches that Dr. Eubanks could have attended that evening. Some might have criticized him for "wasting his time" on a congregation who, at the most, could make a minimal contribution to the campaign.

The president, however, did not think this way. He warmly thanked the congregation for their support in the past, noting the church's long and distinguished history in support of the college. He presented the campaign's goals and made his appeal for sacrificial giving as if this was a congregation of five hundred instead of fifty members. In fact, he apologized to the group for not visiting "his own backyard" earlier in the campaign. Two worthwhile causes were helped that evening: the college received a pledge for the centennial campaign, and the self-esteem of a small, struggling church was greatly bolstered.

Following the death of President Bell in February, 1968, the trustees appointed Dr. Floyd E. Clark as Acting Executive Vice-President of Johnson Bible College. Dr. Clark was a native of Saskatchewan, Canada and came to J.B.C. as a student in 1937. Upon graduation in 1941, he enrolled at Butler School of Religion and graduated in 1944. Dr. Clark returned to Johnson Bible College in that year as Professor of Greek and New Testament and was appointed Dean of the college in 1946.

Dean Clark's zeal for evangelism and dedication to hard work was evident from his student days at J.B.C. He was instrumental in establishing an inner city mission in Knoxville. He served as minister of several churches in the Knoxville area, including a highly successful ministry with the First Christian Church in Maryville, Tennessee. Clark was instrumental in the success of the Smoky Mountain Men's Fellowship in establishing new churches in the region. He conducted almost one hundred Elders and Deacons Clinics across the United States and Canada. Dean Clark has written and produced several Christian dramas, including "The Everlasting Arms," which had over two hundred performances by J.B.C. students in the United States and Canada. He may be best remembered by work students at Johnson as a tireless supervisor during the construction of several college buildings.

Floyd Clark married Lillian "Billie" Frazier in 1941. Mrs. Clark taught at Gap Creek Elementary School for thirty-one years and was a beloved member of the Kimberlin Heights community as well as the college family. Dr. and Mrs. Clark established Sunny Hills Children's Home in Knoxville (near the J.B.C. campus) and Mrs. Clark served as director of the home from 1961-76.

Dean Clark guided the college through an exacting year after the death of President Bell. In addition to continuing Dr. Bell's heavy load of correspondence, Dr. Clark supervised the completion of necessary details that were essential to the transition to a new administration. He retained his duties as Academic Dean and ably adjusted teaching assignments for the 1968-69 term. He supervised the construction of the sewage treatment plant and system which was installed in the summer of 1968. His own evaluation of circumstances at the college during this period was certainly valid: "the Faculty is responding nobly to added responsibilities and student morale is high." In honor of Dean Clark's service as Executive Vice-President and his years of service to the college and the Church, the trustees of Johnson Bible College awarded him the Doctor of Divinity degree in 1969. One year later Dr. Clark received the Johnson Bible College Distinguished Service Award, given annually by the Alumni Association. He retired as Academic Dean in 1974 and continued his teaching duties until his "retirement" in May, 1979.

Dr. David Lawson Eubanks became the fifth president of Johnson Bible College on February 12, 1969, succeeding the late Robert M. Bell. He had served as professor at the school since 1958—teaching history, literature, and Bible—and was well-known to faculty, students, alumni, and friends of the college. Born on November 18, 1935, in Knoxville, Eubanks moved with his family to nearby Maryville, Tennessee. He was a member of First Christian Church, Maryville, under the preaching ministry of Floyd E. Clark. After graduating valedictorian of his high school class, he dedicated himself to full-time Christian service and enrolled at Johnson Bible College in the fall of 1953.

Eubanks completed the Bachelor of Arts degree in 1957 (Magna Cum Laude) and received the Master of Theology from the college one year later. He began teaching at Johnson Bible College in 1958 and also enrolled at the University of Tennessee, earning the Bachelor of Science degree in 1960 and the Doctor of Philosophy degree in history in 1965.

While he distinguished himself as a student, Dr. Eubanks was involved in ministry. He began a "week-end" ministry with the Christian Church in Artemus, Kentucky, during his freshman year at the college and remained with that congregation until the winter of his senior year. He was instrumental in the establishment of the Woodlawn Christian Church in Knoxville, serving as its minister from 1956 until his acceptance of the presidency. Under his leadership the Woodlawn congregation experienced steady numerical growth, developed an increasing missionary commitment program, and completed construction of two new buildings for worship and education.

Dr. Eubanks married Margaret Joyce Perry, also a graduate

of the college, in December, 1955. The Eubanks family that moved into the White House in 1969 also included sons David, Jr. and Philip, and daughter Linnie. Mrs. Eubanks has continued the tradition of gracious hospitality in the presidential home. Her ministry to college guests, faculty, staff, and students through dinners and receptions has been warmly received. Her dramatic presentations have provided a memorable personal touch to many of these occasions.

Although some dissension is expected when a position of this magnitude is concerned, few questioned David Eubanks' qualifications for the presidency of Johnson Bible College. He clearly understood the purpose of the college, was committed to its ideals, had experience in its daily operation, and had demonstrated his capabilities as a preacher and teacher. He understood the tremendous responsibility he had undertaken: "I would be dishonest if I did not say that I . . . believe that the position to which I have been called is a sacred and influential one . . .."[1]

President Eubanks did not enter his term under the kind of duress which greeted every one of his predecessors. Ashley and Emma Johnson, Alva Ross Brown, and Robert Bell faced almost insurmountable odds in the first years of their administration (Dr. Bell called it his "seven years of purgatory"). Overcoming such formidable obstacles in often dramatic ways has evoked great sympathy and respect for those involved. Any friend of the college would empathize with the Johnsons as they fervently prayed for money to refill the pasteboard box out of which they paid the daily bills; or young Alva Ross Brown's struggle to keep the doors open in the midst of the Depression; or Robert Bell's desperate pleas for funds to rescue the college from the brink of bankruptcy. David Eubanks was not met with those kinds of dramatic problems. There was no excessively long deliberation or uncertainty in his selection by the trustees. The college was in the best financial condition in its history. Its buildings were in good repair. Its faculty was loyal and capable. Student enrollment during Dr. Bell's final year was the highest ever and showed no signs of decline.

This is not to imply that Dr. Eubanks stepped into a "cushy" job with few problems. The office of President of Johnson Bible College carries a tremendous burden of responsibility for not only securing the financial resources necessary for operation, but also maintaining the ideals of the college and its service to the church. The obstacles facing him were more subtle—less obvious to supporters that often had to be convinced of their magnitude. The negative consequences of these problems were just as dangerous to the future of the institution as those more easily recognized. These issues facing the Eubanks administration were directly related to the social changes in American society from the late sixties to the present. They may be summarized under the general themes of changes in the character of American higher education and the American churches.

Government involvement in higher education began escalating in the late sixties and became entrenched in the seventies. Federal and state-sponsored grants and loans for education fostered more government regulation of colleges and universities. Accreditation became an essential ingredient of the relationship between the government and the small college to guarantee that students would receive the widely available financial aid. Accreditation demanded increased organization, planning, and accountability within the institution. Johnson Bible College's traditional isolation from government regulation and aversion toward accreditation would be seriously challenged.

The character of college students also changed during the last two decades. More older students, especially married ones, returned to college. Many of these enrolled with previous college experience and degrees. More students pursued graduate degrees—the four-year Bachelors degree is often considered inadequate for a professional career. Many graduate students with Bible college degrees attended state universities as well as seminaries. A standardized curriculum and recognition by regional accreditation associations are necessary to engender the pursuit of advanced degrees. Competition for students has dramatically increased in the past decade. The "baby boom" generation's inundation of colleges and universities in the mid-to-late-sixties has been replaced by a dearth of college-age students—a trend that demographers predict will continue for some time. This has required institutions of higher learning to expand public relations and recruiting efforts.

Educational philosophy has also changed in the past two

decades. The advent of the widely available personal computer
has increased the amount of accessible information and encouraged a more independent approach to learning. Pressures
upon colleges and universities to develop more pragmatic, vo-
cationally oriented programs has led to a decrease of liberal
arts courses and an expansion of specialized ones. A "con-
sumer" mentality permeates the student body, which views the
educational institution as "selling a product" for which the student pays dearly. "Student Satisfaction" has become an important category for college assessment investigators and
therefore a key concern of college administrators.

The economic recessions of the mid-seventies and late-eight-
ies have placed great pressure on colleges. The state universities have seen significant reductions in funding and have
turned to private contributors to provide a higher percentage
of the institution's income. Private colleges and universities
have felt an even greater financial crunch. Financial development offices have been forced to be creative in approaches to
securing gifts. Endowments, investments, trusts, estate planning, and scholarship programs have become essential to the
survival of the small college. Because of the competition for the
generous donor, institutions must demonstrate sound financial
management, accountability, and planning. Whereas most of
these requirements would have been "good ideas" in the past,
they are absolute necessities in the contemporary world of
higher education.

One significant development that has particularly influenced the churches of the Restoration heritage and has directly
challenged the traditional purpose and philosophy of Johnson
Bible College is an enlarged concept of ministry. Reflecting recent theological emphases on the "priesthood of all believers,"
"spiritual gifts," and "every-member ministry," the churches
have broadened their definition of what constitutes full-time
Christian service. The professional staff of the local church in
many cases goes well beyond the "preacher" and includes ex-
perts in the fields of education, youth ministry, counseling,
campus ministry, family ministry, music, and seniors ministry
(to name but a few). This enlarged concept of ministry also en-
compasses various missionary enterprises (stateside and overseas), social agencies, and educational institutions. One

controversial aspect of this development is the changing role of women in American society and the American church: to what extent will women be included in the professional ministry of the local church? How can a college that has traditionally been a "Preacher-Training Institution in a Preacher-Growing Atmosphere" adjust to a concept of ministry that seems to diminish the role of the preacher?

In an excellent study of how small, church-related colleges survive under contemporary pressures such as those described above, Gerald Tiffin and Phillip Robinette identified three essential "keys to survival":

1. Identification of environmental changes and possible college responses.
2. Faithfulness to a specialized purpose.
3. Sensitivity to a well-defined, loyal constituency.[2]

President Eubanks and his administration discovered these principles in the crucible of experience. Johnson Bible College's impressive growth since 1968 may be traced to Dr. Eubanks' awareness and implementation of these keys.

In his inauguration speech on May 23, 1969, President Eubanks pledged himself to the historic purpose of the school:

This college was founded primarily to train ministers of the gospel. We do not criticize in any way our church-related schools which specialize in other fields, but we still want Johnson to be known for educating and inspiring faithful and challenging preachers.[3]

He recognized, however, certain adjustments the college must make. He affirmed his support for female students and promised "to do everything we can to frame a curriculum for them which will allow them to be well trained for Christian service in their own right."[4] He promised to promote academic excellence in the college program and faculty, stating that this is "not inconsistent with personal commitment or faithfulness to the Word of God."[5] His monumental task was to engender these "adjustments" without altering the college's historic purpose. The current purpose statement reflects this balance: "The purpose of Johnson Bible College is to educate students for specialized Christian ministries with emphasis on the preaching ministry."[6]

President Eubanks has identified the "environmental changes" the college is facing and has clearly articulated his general response. Writing in the *Christian Standard* on two separate occasions, Dr. Eubanks noted the twin problems of increased costs for education and the decrease in number of available students. In "The Cost of a Qualified Ministry," Dr. Eubanks admitted that J.B.C.'s philosophy of keeping student charges low, remaining a single-purpose institution, and recruiting more married students intensified these problems. He listed a number of strategies to which Johnson Bible College was committed: a clearly understood and articulated mission; good institutional planning; sound management; deep commitment on the part of the faculty and staff; creative recruitment of students; special accommodation of married students; and diversified giving programs.[7]

Under the insightful leadership of President Eubanks, Johnson Bible College has nearly doubled the size of the student body, conducted several highly successful financial campaigns, completed four major buildings and two major renovations of existing buildings, become a pioneer for Bible Colleges in the area of accreditation, and developed an innovative curriculum and well-qualified faculty. During his term in office (1969-present) annual gift income has increased by seven hundred and forty percent and the overall endowment by twelve hundred percent. Johnson Bible College has become a model for similar institutions within and beyond the Restoration Movement. In the past twenty-three years the growth of the college has reflected the steadfastness of Dr. Eubanks' self-assessed personality: "I am not by nature an alarmist. I am more of a 'plodder.' My inclination is to move on with determination, trusting God to supply what is lacking."[8]

Enrollment of students at J.B.C. has followed an upward track with only brief periods of decline. After an enrollment of 235 students in 1969, the college experienced two acute increases: from 238 in 1972 to 303 the following year and from 332 in 1974 to 438 in 1975. The former escalation coincided with the opening of new dormitories and the latter with the Phillips-Welshimer multi-purpose building. After a record enrollment of 442 in 1976, the student body fluctuated in the

370-390 range from 1978 through 1987. The past four years have seen a renewed surge in enrollment, with records set in 1991 (470 students; this includes 43 graduate students) and 1992 (488 students; this includes 50 graduate students). This surge may reflect a response to the construction of the Eubanks Activity Center and the major addition to the library.

The increase in enrollment has been accompanied by an increase in the percentage of married and female students. Dr. Eubanks' 1981 college report to the *Christian Standard* included a note that approximately one-third of the 404 students at J.B.C. were married.[9] In 1984 (when dependable statistics recording married students became available) there were 100 married students out of a total enrollment of 374 (28%). This percentage has remained fairly constant until the present time (the 24% figure for 1991 has been the lowest). The 1969 class included 93 females (40% of total student body); this percentage increased to 44% in 1975 and averaged 46% from 1976-1991. Approximately one-fourth of the female students were married. Very few of the students from 1969-1991 were from African-American, Native American, Hispanic, or Oriental ethnic origins.

Many things have changed the experience of students on the Johnson Bible College campus in the past twenty-five years. The isolation of the campus has decreased significantly with the growth of the South Knoxville and Seymour communities. Most students drive their own vehicles. The farm operation no longer exists (with the exception of a few cattle) and the work program centers around college services and maintenance of facilities. Students experience few inconveniences in the classroom and dormitory and have access to more than adequate educational and recreational resources.

A wide variety of student activities, however, remain an important component of the J.B.C. experience. The literary societies have been replaced by special-interest groups such as Harvesters (missions) and Quest (youth ministry), and the Timothy Club still provides opportunities for "practice preaching." Music groups such as the J.B.C. Choir, New Encounter, and Declaration have traveled to churches, conventions, and Christian camps all over the United States (and included a trip to Europe in 1988). Students are involved in weekend preaching, youth, and music ministries in churches throughout the region. The Christian Service program encourages student participation with a variety of agencies and organizations in the Knoxville area such as jail ministry, hospital chaplaincy, counseling centers, ministry to senior citizens, and inner city ministry to children. The successful intercollegiate sports program—men's basketball, soccer, and baseball and women's basketball and volleyball—provides an important diversion from the rigorous academic schedule. The "Preacher Grand Prix" (an annual wagon race with competition between the classes), intramural sports activities, hayrides, bonfires, "hootenannies," Founder's Day, and "porch sings" are meaningful components of student life.

The escalation of the number of students required the expansion of the facilities of the college. Dr. Bell and friend of Johnson, Allen Buzard, had planned to challenge the alumni at the 1968 Homecoming to raise one and a half "Millions for the Master" toward a teachers' salary endowment fund and the contruction of a new dormitory. Following Dr. Bell's death during that Homecoming, the campaign was carried on in his memory. Not one, but two, dormitories were subsequently built (Alva Ross Bown Hall for men, 1971; and Emma Elizabeth Johnson Hall for women, 1972), and the Millions for the Master Fund to augment faculty salaries became a part of the college endowment.

The B.D. Phillips Charitable Trust generously provided funding for the two and one quarter million dollar Phillips-Welshimer Multi-purpose Building, dedicated on August 24, 1975. This building incorporated classrooms, faculty and administrative offices, gymnasium, cafeteria, and student center into a central facility. It also changed the complexion of the campus—replacing Old Main as the principal building and requiring the demolition of the massive barn that had greeted visitors to the college for seventy-five years. Recognizing the pressing need to accommodate the expanding number of married students, a "Housing for Future Harvesters" campaign was launched Thanksgiving, 1978, with a goal to raise $450,000 by December 31, 1981. The goal was exceeded and was used to renovate the apartments in Bell Hall and build a number of duplexes for married student housing. Operation

Renovate raised $300,000 to remodel Old Main and the old Boys Dormitory, which was completed in two phases. The Carl O. Hoffmann Center for Special Services (which currently houses the graduate program) was dedicated in September, 1981, followed by the dedication of Floyd E. Clark Hall (men's dormitory) in 1985. The successful "Invest in Tomorrow" campaign procured $1.5 million from 1984-88 to enlarge the permanent funding of the college.

The most ambitious financial campaign in the history of the college was announced by President Eubanks at the 1988 Homecoming. A six-year, six million dollar capital fund drive, entitled "Centennial: A Celebration of Service," would culminate at the end of the centennial year. This campaign, which grew out of a several months' long self-examination and institutional planning session, would include the construction of an activities center, major addition to the library, additional married student housing, upgrading of telephone, computer, video, and printing equipment, renovation of classrooms, offices, and cafeteria, and an increase of permanent funding for the college. By the next Homecoming (February 1989) eighty percent of the six million dollar goal had been pledged with almost nine hundred thousand dollars already received. The Eubanks Activities Center was dedicated on February 15, 1990, followed by the completion of a major addition to the existing library. By August 31, 1991, the six million dollars goal was exceeded in pledges (with over 3.5 million dollars received). The trustees decided to extend the campaign goal to seven million dollars with full expectation of achieving the goal.

There were other significant improvements to the physical plant in addition to construction associated with the major campaigns. At least eleven houses and duplexes were built for faculty and staff. New shop and warehouse facilities were constructed to accommodate the expanding maintenance department. Much effort has been expended to beautify the campus grounds with extensive landscaping projects.

One factor that has significantly contributed to these financial achievements is the continued role of the alumni of the college though the Alumni Association and the Council of Seventy. The Board of Trustees was also expanded (allowing ten to twelve members) and included more members from the business and professional fields. Great effort was made, however, to follow Dr. Johnson's instructions that the trustees should be members of the Christian Church and that a majority should be alumni of the college.

Another reason for the success of these campaigns was the increase of programs for friends of the college. The annual Women's Retreat was initiated in 1972 and has recently drawn nearly five hundred women to the campus each spring. One of the most popular current programs is the Senior Saints in the Smokies. This week-long program of Bible study, workshops, and recreation has steadily grown to include nearly seven hundred "senior saints" and expanded to three weeks in 1992.

Johnson Bible College has maintained its tradition of providing work for the student who is unable to pay for his or her education, although the nature of the "work program" has changed a great deal in the past two decades. Work-study is included in a financial aid "package" that also involves government grants and loans, and a large number of J.B.C. scholarships. Most students still work in the campus program but not to the extent of students under previous administrations. Dr. Eubanks has frankly explained that the current configuration of the work-study program costs the school a considerable amount of money, but he has no plans to deviate from the college's traditional commitment to help "the poor young man."

Another of Johnson Bible College's adjustments to meet contemporary challenges has been its active pursuit of accreditation. In the same *Blue and White* that contained Dr. Eubanks' Inauguration Address was the announcement of an institutional self-study which would lead to accreditation by the Accrediting Association of Bible Colleges (AABC).[10] J.B.C. received full accreditation from the AABC on March 6, 1970. By 1976 the college was also a member of the Tennessee College Association and the Tennessee Council of Private Colleges and had applied for accreditation with the Commission on Colleges of the Southern Association of Colleges and Schools (SACS, the major regional accrediting association for all institutions of higher learning). Cautiously diffusing opposition to this process, Dr. Eubanks and Academic Dean William R. Blevins coordinated the completion of the requirements for full accreditation by the

Southern Association in December, 1979, with J.B.C. becoming one of the first two Bible Colleges accredited by that body.

The administration was very careful to explain that accreditation did not affect the college's purpose or the Bible-centered curriculum and that it would not lead to excessive government intrusion and regulation. The January 1980 *Blue and White* contained a lengthy explanation of these concerns:

> There are people who seem to confuse higher education accreditation and government regulation. In America higher education accreditation is by voluntary associations of colleges and universities. Standards are set, and schools are evaluated by themselves and by committees of their peers. The accrediting associations have been among the most outspoken critics of government intrusion and regulation in higher education. . . . In our case peer evaluation was free from any recommendations or changes in the sensitive areas of purpose, spiritual and moral commitment of the faculty, or the Bible curriculum. . . . There was never a suggestion that the college hire faculty members who were not committed to Christ, his church, and the principles of the Restoration Movement. There was no recommendation to alter the Bible curriculum. . . . Johnson Bible College remains committed to its historic purpose and mission of educating students for Christian service here and overseas.[11]

These assurances were also published in the *Christian Standard*.[12] President Eubanks served as the President of the AABC (which represents over 250 Bible Colleges in North America) in 1981. Dean Blevins (and other J.B.C. personnel) continues to serve on SACS and AABC evaluation committees.

Enforcement of the standards of the AABC and SACS has required the development of an ongoing assessment and planning process. The assumption of the administration is that this process is essential to the future development of the college and should be incorporated whether required or not. Accreditation has also fostered improvements in the library facilities, higher qualification standards for faculty members, and a stronger curriculum—especially in biblical and general studies. It has also enabled graduates to pursue advanced university and seminary degrees with little or no prerequisites.

The academic program also underwent a major change in 1978. The curriculum had become somewhat confused by the number of degree options that had evolved. Specialized programs in missions, teacher education, nursing, and secretarial work had been "tacked on" to the existing scheme. Some of these were cooperative degrees with the University of Tennessee and the Baptist Hospital School of Nursing. This system was simplified in 1978 by the adoption of a core curriculum with a Bible major (Bachelor of Arts—which required two years of Greek—or Bachelor of Science) and a choice of nine specialty areas (commonly called a minor). Reflecting the broadening concept of ministry within the churches and providing widening opportunities for female students, these specialties included preaching, youth ministry, missions, music, Christian education, special education, communications, secretarial, and home economics. The list of specialties has been refined throughout the 1980s, dropping the secretarial and home economics programs and adding computers, deaf ministry, and counseling.

The current specialties include: preaching, missions, youth ministry and preaching, Christian education, telecommunications, deaf missions, youth ministry and Christian education, counseling, and teaching English to speakers of other languages. Double-major B.S. programs are offered in Bible and Teacher Education (with full state certification for grades K–8), Bible and Church Music, and Bible and Nursing. Under this new curriculum students are required to complete a minimum of 30 semester credits in Bible, 18-21 credits in their specialty area, and the remainder in general studies and electives.

Considerable effort has been expended by the Eubanks faculty and administration to maintain the college's emphasis on the preaching ministry. An analysis of the graduates from 1984-1992 reveals that fifty-four percent of the male students graduated under the preaching or missions specialties. A graduate program offering a thirty semester hour Master of Arts in New Testament Exposition and Research or New Testament Exposition and Preaching was inaugurated in 1988. This degree may be completed by residence or video correspondence. The graduate program has been accredited by the Commission on Colleges Southern Association of Colleges and Schools.

Another area in which the Eubanks administration has seen dramatic change is in the educational qualifications of faculty members. When Dr. Eubanks became president in 1969 only two faculty members held earned doctorates—himself and Dr. Blevins. Eleven of the twenty full-time teaching faculty members in 1991 held earned doctorates. This development has been accompanied by an increase in faculty salaries, benefits, and supportive equipment and facilities. Academic Dean William Blevins has been largely responsible for the development of standardized faculty contracts, rank requirements, and evaluation procedures. Faculty members must affirm the doctrinal position of Johnson Bible College which acknowledges belief in the existence of "one true God of the Old and New Testaments"; the inspiration and all-sufficiency of the Old and New Testaments; the deity, virgin birth, and all-sufficiency of the work of Christ; His atoning death and bodily resurrection; the priority of the Great Commission; the work of the Holy Spirit; the necessity of faith, repentance, confession, and baptism (immersion) for salvation; commitment to the Restoration Plea for church unity through obedience to the authority of the New Testament; and the return of Christ to judge the nations. The *Faculty and Administration Guidebook* states:

> No person shall ever be elected to serve as Trustee, Teacher, or in any other faculty or administrative position, who is not in accord with the Doctrinal Position of the College.

> Any such person who shall be found to be out of harmony with the Doctrinal Position as stated above, shall be constitutionally out of office upon proof of his or her disqualification and shall no longer be regarded as a representative of Johnson Bible College.[13]

This affirmation of faith in the fundamental doctrines of the Christian faith is one way that Johnson Bible College has expressed historical continuity with its foundational purpose and beliefs.

One cannot mention the Johnson Bible College faculty during President Eubanks' years without special recognition of the teaching career of Dr. Robert E. Black. Dr. Black was employed by Johnson Bible College longer than any other person in the history of the school (1949-89). Following graduation from Johnson and Butler School of Religion, Robert Black returned to J.B.C. in August of 1949 to serve on the faculty, teaching in the area of Old Testament. Dr. Black's "key questions," quizzes, and lively lectures provided a thorough understanding of the Old Testament to appreciative students. He was the minister of the Lonsdale Christian Church in Knoxville for twenty-eight years. In addition to his classroom teaching and preaching, he also played a key role in the development of the college's Correspondence Department and served for several years as the Dean of Students. In recognition of his service he was awarded by his alma mater the Johnson Bible College Alumni Distinguished Service Award and an honorary Doctor of Divinity degree. Dr. Black died in October, 1989. He taught a Bible school class at Lonsdale on the Sunday morning before his death—an appropriate tribute to this popular, dedicated, and influential man.

Under President Eubanks' leadership Johnson Bible College has maintained an important position within the Bible college movement throughout the nation. The oldest Bible college within the Christian Church/Churches of Christ, J.B.C. has been a pioneer in the area of accreditation, curriculum development, financial campaign strategies, and assessment and planning. The 1991-92 report on Christian colleges in the *Christian Standard* listed Johnson as the fifth largest Bible college among the Independents with the third highest annual total gift income. This has been accomplished in spite of a limited local support base for fund-raising and recruitment of students when compared to larger colleges.

The Eubanks era at Johnson Bible College has seen great emphasis placed upon the history and tradition of the college. Founder's Day has become a forum for long-time associates of the college to relate their memories of experiences on the Hill. The *Blue and White* published a well-received series of insightful historical anecdotes entitled "Echoes From the Hill" and continues to give historical material a prominent place. There has been a concentrated effort to collect and preserve historical photographs and memorabilia. Mrs. Eubanks expressed this sense of appreciation for tradition by quoting Phillips Brooks in her response to the 1984 Homecoming tribute to President Eubanks and herself: "The place where true friends met is sacred to them all through their friendship, all the more sacred as their friendship deepens and grows old."[14]

Dr. Eubanks received an honorary Doctor of Divinity degree

from the college in 1984 in recognition of his vital service as president. Mrs. Eubanks' contribution was also honored with the presentation of an automobile. Dr. Eubanks continues to hold a high place of respect within the churches of the Restoration Movement as author, educator, and preacher. He has served as president of the North American Christian Convention and remains heavily involved in various missionary endeavors.

This chapter does not end with the death of a president of Johnson Bible College. Instead of looking back to a "home-going," one may look forward to a "Homecoming"—the centennial celebration. Plans have been made to welcome over one thousand guests to the annual Homecoming and Preaching Rally in February, 1993. A special service has been arranged for Founder's Day on May 12, 1993, the one hundredth anniversary of the laying of the cornerstone of the first Main Building. Although most graduates and alumni from the past would not recognize much of the current campus, they would pause and reflect upon a familiar marble stone set in the doorway of Old Main on which are inscribed familiar words to any friend of Johnson Bible College:

SCHOOL OF
THE EVANGELISTS

FOUNDED 1893 - REBUILT 1905

OPEN DAY AND NIGHT TO
THE POOR YOUNG MAN WHO
DESIRES ABOVE EVERY OTHER
DESIRE TO PREACH THE
GOSPEL OF CHRIST.

ASHLEY S. JOHNSON
EMMA E. JOHNSON
KIMBERLIN HEIGHTS, TENN.
JUNE 22, 1905

ROBT. M. IRWIN, BUILDER

David L. Eubanks,
High School Graduation

David L. Eubanks,
Johnson Bible College Junior

President David L. Eubanks, 1969

President David L. Eubanks, 1990

Professor David L. Eubanks at his classroom desk, c. 1965

Dr. Eubanks receiving the presidential seal from trustee chairman, A. Berton Clarke, 1969

1981 Senior Class President Jeff Noel presenting Thanksgiving offering to Dr. Eubanks

President Eubanks at his Phillips-Welshimer building office, 1982

David and Margaret Eubanks, c. 1965

David and Margaret Eubanks with their children,
David, Jr., Linnie, and Phillip, 1987

David and Margaret Eubanks, 1991

The Eubanks Family (with grandchildren), 1991

Margaret (Perry) Eubanks as a JBC student, c. 1955

Mrs. David (Margaret) Eubanks at a White House reception

Margaret Eubanks receiving her new car with Phillip, Linnie and David, Jr. at the Eubanks' tribute, Homecoming, 1984

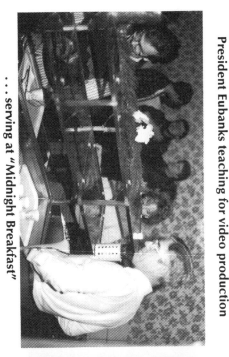

President Eubanks teaching for video production

. . . serving at "Midnight Breakfast"

. . . speaking to a church group

. . . playing football with the "campus kids"

President Eubanks in Zambia, Africa, with Dean and Judy Davis, 1973

President and Mrs. Eubanks with George Bajenski and students from the Correspondence Bible Seminary near Warsaw, Poland, 1986

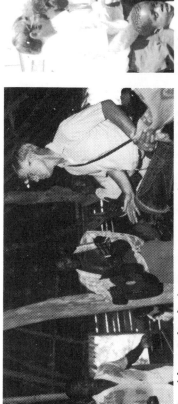

President Eubanks in Papua New Guinea on a visit to John and Bonita Pryor, 1988

President and Mrs. Eubanks with Ruth Sanders and church members in Brazil, 1986

Emma S. Johnson Hall (Women's Dormitory) — Dedicated August, 1972

Eubanks Activity Center — Dedicated 1991

Alva Ross Brown Hall (Men's Dormitory) — Dedicated February, 1971

Married student housing at Gateway Court

Aerial view of the 1991 campus

Trustee Mildred Welshimer Phillips "breaks ground" for the Phillips-Welshimer Building, 1972

Phillips-Welshimer Multi-purpose Building — Dedicated August, 1975

The cupola from "Old Main" was removed July 26, 1974, and reposi-
tioned on top of the new Phillips-Welshimer Building on October 21. The
bell, which had been used to signal the beginning and end of campus
events since 1905, was placed in a beautiful brick marker in front of the
new building.

Trustees 1976: (Back) Cannaday, Bealle, Hackett, McKowen, Musick, Kineman, Wheeler (Front) Reid, Phillips, Eubanks, Fulton, Hasty

Honored dignitaries and faculty prepare for the inauguration of David L. Eubanks, 1969

1978 JBC Administrators: Wilbur Reid, Jr., William R. Blevins, President Eubanks, John M. Lowe, Ben D. Lutz, Robert Jones

Johnson Bible College Trustees, 1987: Fulton, Eubanks, Bennett, Martin, (back) Coleman, Hasty, Carnathan, Campbell, and Overdorf

"Mayberry JBC" program performed by faculty and staff at the 1990 Miller-Scott Christmas Banquet

Faculty and staff serving "Midnight Breakfast" to the students during final exams, 1985

Faculty and staff at the 1987 reception for Freshman students

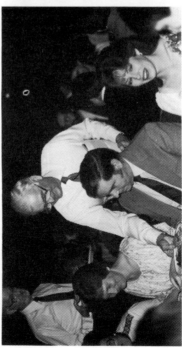

Professor Bob Martin and Stafford Davis serve students at the 1982 Miller-Scott Christmas Banquet.

1991–92 JBC Faculty at the Faculty-Staff Christmas Dinner

Class of 1991 on the Brown Hall steps

Robert Black, professor for 35 years, and Edith Snow, dean of women for 20 years, received the Alumni Distinguished Service Award — 1969

Dr. and Mrs. Black in his final Freshman reception line

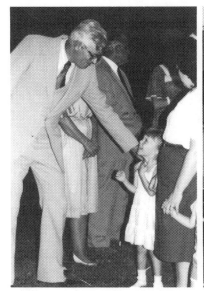

Professor Lee Richardson has served on the faculty since 1957

Professor Gary Weedman in a homiletics class, 1971

The first JBC Homecoming — May 22, 1923

Phillip Sams leading a workshop at 1983 Homecoming

1970 Homecoming services in Alumni Chapel

Class of 1945 at their 40th year reunion, 1985

1986 Erosthe service

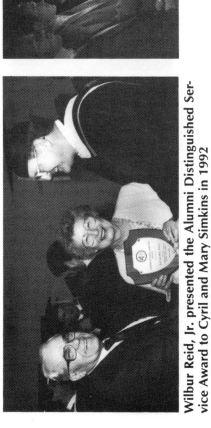

Wilbur Reid, Jr. presented the Alumni Distinguished Service Award to Cyril and Mary Simkins in 1992

1976 Commemcement, Phillips-Welshimer Auditorium

Dr. and Mrs. Eubanks with Barry and Edna McLean (niece of Ashley S. Johnson)

Dr. and Mrs Eubanks entertaining guests in the White House dining room

Dr. and Mrs. Eubanks with Mrs. Alva Ross Brown, 1989

Myrtle Bell, Mildred Phillips, and Alma Brown at a White House luncheon, c. 1980

Kathryn Watts speaking at the Eubanks Tribute, Homecoming, 1984

Dr. Beauford Bryant at the 1992 Homecoming

Madonna Burget, Ginny and Bill Loft receiving Alumni Distinguished Service Award, 1984

The 1977 Declaration singing group preparing to "hit the road"

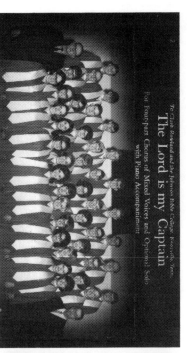

The JBC Choir — 1970

The New Encounter — 1980

Madrigal Singers — 1985

JBC Cheerleaders, 1969: Carol Bowers, Bob Stevens, Mary Followell, John Simmons, Brenda Gill

JBC Preachers competing in the Phillips-Welshimer Gymnasium, 1976

JBC Evangels, District Champions, March 1982

Russell Morgan and his "boys" at dedication of Morgan Field, April 30, 1981. Morgan served as a maintenance supervisor and coached basketball most of the time from 1960 to 1988.

1977 "International Harvesters" missions organization

1984 Thanksgiving Appeal Letter "stuffing"

1972 Student Preachers

Dr. Carl Bridges and students organizing the "Bibles for Brothers" project, 1991

Baling hay on JBC campus, 1991

Phillips-Welshimer Building kitchen, 1979–80

Tearing down the barn, 1968

Mayo Proctor supervising the groundskeeping crew

A view of the French Broad River and Johnson Island from the White House patio, 1991 (same view as pictured on page 34 in 1896)

Aerial view of Glass Memorial Library and Eubanks Activity Center, 1991

Margaret Eubanks, JBC student 1951–55, president's wife 1969 to present

Dr. David L. Eubanks, JBC student 1953–58, professor 1958–69, and president 1969 to present

Current administrators, faculty, and staff who have been at the college twenty years or more. This group represents a total of 356 years of service to the College.

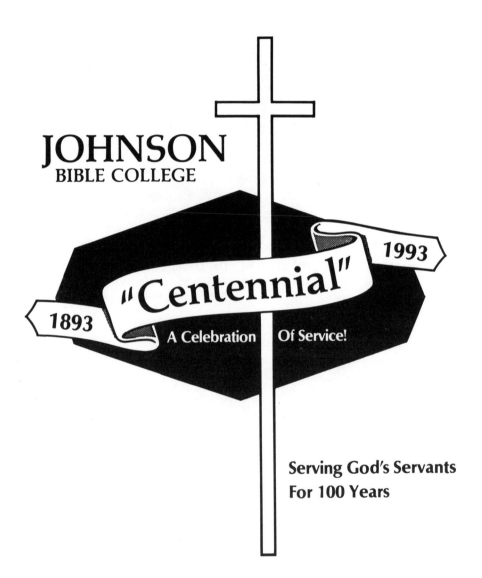

JOHNSON
BIBLE COLLEGE

1893 "Centennial" 1993
A Celebration Of Service!

Serving God's Servants
For 100 Years

EPILOGUE

As one sifts through all of the sources that tell the story of Johnson Bible College—letters, journals, catalogs, books, photographs—one realizes that these are simply shadows, tangible yet fleeting glimpses of past reality. In the words of a student-written introduction to the 1957 J.B.C. annual,

> These are the visible evidences of the spiritual life. But these are only indications and illustrations of a deep sense of dependence, devotion, consecration and love that cannot be photographed but must be experienced. One can know of what the spiritual life of Johnson consists only by living and experiencing it. No physical means can define what is so deeply spiritual.[1]

The "essence" of Johnson Bible College may be summarized in three commitments: to faithfully teach the Word of God, to evangelize the world, and to offer opportunity to the disadvantaged. This brief survey of the history of the college clearly demonstrates that the college—in all its parts—has remained faithful to this "essence," this original vision of its founder. The reason why this institution has such a glorious past and promising future is that, in the words of honored donor and friend B.D. Phillips, Sr., "Johnson Bible College has stuck to its knitting."

This history is incomplete, however, unless it also conveys the "spirit" that underlies these commitments. What has kept attracting students to Johnson Bible College for the past one hundred years? What has bound those students together both on and off campus, as fellow students and faithful alumni? What has inspired them to risk even their lives to fulfill the Great Commission that they learned and dedicated themselves to while at J.B.C.? What has motivated faculty members to invest their time and energies in these students in sacrificial ways? Why have faithful friends of the college given financial and spiritual support in measure far beyond reasonable expectation? Why is there great meaning in the declaration, "He's a Johnson man!"?

There is a common life, a fellowship, shared by Johnson Bible College's students, faculty, administration, trustees, and friends that transcends the years and the campus. It is a fellowship of service in the Kingdom of God. Johnson Bible College has had many notable alumni: Oren E. Long, the first Governor of the State of Hawaii and later Senator from that state; Thornton C. Miller, Rear Admiral of the Navy and the Senior Chaplain in all three military services; Edward Branham, who also served as chaplain in the armed forces and supervised all of the chaplains in the Pacific Theatre during World War II; college and seminary presidents and administrators such as G.H. Cachiaras, Glenn Bourne, D. Ray Lindley, Tibbs Maxey, T.H. Johnson, Harland Cary, Delno Brown, Dean Barr, and Brad Burnette; writers, scholars, and professors such as Fred Craddock, John Ralls, Beauford Bryant, Robert Fife, Frank Albert, Eugene Boring, Ralph Johnson, Howard Short, Cyril C. Simkins, S. Edward Tesh, and Gary Weedman; and pioneer missionaries and Bible translators such as Konstantin Jaroshevich, John J. Hill, John Chase, Harold Hanlin, Harold Taylor, Leslie Wolfe, Charles Sublett, Elmer Kile, Bill Loft, Madonna Burget, L. Dean Davis and C.Y. Kim. Helen Stokes Kerns, Professor of English at J.B.C. for seventeen years, conveyed the sense of pride one feels in the accomplishments of Johnson alumni:

> My, how it thrills my heart to hear some of "my boys" speak on convention programs or read in the Standard articles they have written: Bob Fife, Beauford Bryant, Tibbs Maxey, Ali Jarman, William Tucker, Charles Sublett, Willis Fowler, James McKowen and others.
>
> Some became missionaries: John Hill, Lloyd Sanders, Harold Taylor, Harry Schaefer, Jr., and Harland Cary. Floyd Clark and Robert Black both returned to JBC as professors. Ed Tesh has been teaching at Lincoln Bible College for years. Tibbs Maxey established the College of the Scriptures in Louisville, Kentucky. Ralph Johnson has been at Nebraska Christian College

for 25 years; blind himself, he has taught many to see. Dean
Barr was president of both Dakota and Dallas Bible Colleges.
Charles Matthews, president of Great Lakes Bible College,
now on the staff of Standard. Harland Cary founded Colegio
Biblico. . . .

Oh, I can't begin to name them all. But, when I look at their
pictures in my scrapbook, floods of memories, precious beyond
measure, sweep over me.[2]

The vast majority of Johnson alumni, however, have distinguished themselves in local churches and mission fields where
they have unselfishly and sacrificially served without the acco-
lades of men. In fact, the spirit of Johnson Bible College is best
found in those who are faithfully preaching, teaching, and
serving the needs of people for the cause of Christ without the
desire of recognition and reward. Although some have distinguished themselves in other fields, most have intentionally remained in less prominent places. Ralph Kinney Bennett, senior
editor of the *Reader's Digest*, spoke of these servants in his
1982 commencement address:

When I was a boy I remember going to a men's rally at a
Christian Church somewhere around Pittsburgh, Pennsylvania,
and after the meeting, as we were waiting to board a rented bus
and go back home, I and some other boys were playing on the
steps of the church. I recall that three or four men were standing there talking: What did they think about the qualifications
of this fellow whom they were considering calling to the pulpit
of their church. Well, one qualification of this fellow stood out,
for when it was mentioned the conversation pretty much ceased
in quiet nods of approval. I have always remembered the words,
and the way they were said: "He's a Johnson man."

. . . My impression of this school has come from the Christ-
centered quality of the lives of Johnson alumni. They have
preached the Word, and they have lived it. And the name Johnson Bible College has stood out to me precisely because I have
never known that name to be placed before the name of Christ.

I rub my hands together with anticipation when I'm going to
hear a Johnson man preach. I go expecting preparation. I go expecting scholarship. I go expecting intellect. I get . . . Jesus
Christ and Him crucified. Make no mistake. All the preparation,
the scholarship, the intellect is there, but it has been sublimely
lost in the glory of the Saviour.

What a heritage to live up to. . . . The majority of the people
of this legacy have been largely unknown to human history. . . .

the growth and development of Christ's true Church has been carried out on the shoulders of nameless men and women with the Word laid up in their hearts. Certainly there are names, here and there, emerging from the void—great men and great sermons, magnificent feats of scholarship.. . .

But by and large Christ's work has been done not in the bright light of worldly fame, but in the warm glow of loving hearts; not by the fist pounding the pulpit, but by the gentle hand touching the sick and the lonely.[3]

Johnson Bible College is proud of its alumni who have achieved success, notoriety, and public acclaim. It is equally eager, however, to honor that great number among its ranks who faithfully preach the gospel and serve others in the name of Christ in relative obscurity.

The spirit of Johnson Bible College is also found in its fellowship of thanksgiving. The hard work that has been required to establish and maintain the college and the personal sacrifice demanded of every student who completed the academic program has created a shared sense of gratitude among its alumni. They have toiled for what they have accomplished and are appreciative of those who have worked beside them. The isolation of the college (until the contemporary era) and the daily routine on the farm created a camaraderie among the students that cemented this shared appreciation. Friendships formed at Thanksgiving banquets, founder's days, ballgames, birthday suppers, homecomings, class trips, and long work days have endured across miles and years. When those friendships are accompanied by an understanding of the contributions of many to the life of the college, they are doubly precious.

This fellowship of thanksgiving may be seen in the generosity of alumni Allen Miller and John Scott, who established the "Turkey Fund" to provide the Thanksgiving meal for the students (currently enjoyed as the Miller-Scott Christmas Banquet). The spirit may be seen in Dr. Howard Hayes' memory of his life at J.B.C. in 1924-32:

Each noon the head of the dining room would announce: "Our bread (food) for this day is provided by _____," naming some generous donor, a multitude of whom kept the school going from day to day, and all the students joined in a communal thanksgiving for the generosity by which they lived.[4]

Dr. Hayes concluded his remarks by affirming that "this school had given him an opportunity and a beginning which would not have been available anywhere else." L. D. Campbell's description of his experience at Johnson Bible College echoed that of perhaps thousands of students:

> They took a very poor boy from the mountains of upper East Tennessee and they gave me an opportunity to get one of the finest ministerial trainings in the country. While there I was surrounded with people who saw potential in me that I never saw in myself.[5]

The spirit of Johnson Bible College is a fellowship in truth. The college has unashamedly remained a "Bible" college. The adage "If he's from Johnson, he can preach," has been sounded in churches throughout the brotherhood because of Johnson's commitment to teaching the Word of God and to thorough preparation for ministry. The Senior Class of 1954 wrote:

> From the time that we signed our names to the Johnson ledger in enrollment, we have been exhorted to strive toward a great goal in truthfulness. This goal, "If a Johnson man says it, it's true," has ever been impressed on our minds. For this reason the curriculum of the college has been based on the unchanging truth of God's Word.[6]

Finally, it is a fellowship in prayer. The Fiftieth Anniversary Class of 1943 expressed it as follows:

> One feature of Johnson Bible College is the fellowship of student with student and student with teacher. The constant fellowship in study, work, worship, and play makes a bond of brotherhood which will never be dissolved. The discussion-type classes and the comparative isolation of the campus beget a fraternal spirit which is sealed in the evening prayer meeting.[7]

There is a unique expression of spirituality embodied in the slogan, "Faith, Prayer, and Work." That spirituality was institutionalized at J.B.C. in the prayer room and the evening prayer meeting (chapel). Ashley S. Johnson's deep trust in God and confident prayer life is intrinsic to the J.B.C. experience. Classes begin with prayer. The daily chapel services include a significant amount of time devoted to prayer. The faculty gathers regularly to pray. Numerous student groups have appointed times for prayer. The prayer room in Old Main still welcomes several students and faculty members every day. The annual prayer chain is held in November to accompany the Thanksgiving appeal letters. All of the activities of the college are bathed in prayer. The Senior Class of 1949 recorded their experience of this fellowship:

> This year's ceaseless prayer program continued for three weeks. A fitting climax to this inspirational season is reached on Thanksgiving Day, with a special Thanksgiving service, the presentation of the check by the senior class to President Bell, the turkey dinner—made possible by John Scott of Tennessee, and the annual Gravy Bowl football game in the afternoon between the societies. Truly, we as seniors are more thankful to Him who gives every good and perfect gift, because we have spent four Thanksgiving seasons at J.B.C.[8]

The best summary of the spirit of Johnson Bible College, especially concerning its fellowship in prayer, is by Ashley S. Johnson. It is fitting that this book concludes with his words:

What is Johnson Bible College?

It might be better to ask, "Who is Johnson Bible College?" The answer to either question depends entirely upon the standpoint from which you view it. One driving out from the city of Knoxville and suddenly coming in sight of Kimberlin Heights would probably be much surprised at the splendid buildings which have been erected here in answer to prayer and might say: "That is Johnson Bible College." If after arrival a visitor should be introduced to the young preachers and attend our prayer meeting, he might say: "These are Johnson Bible College." If, however, I should take him to our Prayer Chamber on the fourth floor of the main building and show him the photographs of our friends, on the walls of the chamber, and show him also a list of the Brothers and Sisters in Christ representing a large portion of the English-speaking world, who pray for us and work with us, he might say, and with much truth: "These are Johnson Bible College," for without these friends the work could not live. Johnson Bible College, therefore, is not bounded by brick walls, by state lines, or by national lines. It is rather a great company of believers unknown to each other in the flesh or even by name, fired by the same spirit, giving their hearts and lives to one great end. Whoever views Johnson Bible

College from any view-point save our Chamber of Prayer will of necessity have a limited view of its principles, of its purposes, of its objects . . . [and] of the great company of believers bound together in the great resolve to send forth laborers into the harvest.[9]

END NOTES

CHAPTER ONE, Pages 19–30

1. Ashley S. Johnson, "The Story of One Hundred Dollars" (Knoxville: Ogden Brothers and Co., 1900), p. 4.

2. Alva Ross Brown, *Standing on the Promises* (Knoxville: S.B. Newman and Co., 1928), p. 171.

3. Ashley S. Johnson, "The Story of a Check for One Hundred Dollars" (Knoxville: Ogden Brothers and Co., 1900), p. 8.

4. Ibid., pp. 8-9.

5. Ashley S. Johnson, *Johnson Bible College Newsletter* (October 1916), p. 1.

6. Johnson, "Story of a Check," p. 9.

7. Ibid.

8. Ibid. See also C.C. Ware, *South Carolina Disciples of Christ: A History* (Charleston: Christian Churches of South Carolina, 1967), p. 51.

9. Herman A. Norton, *Religion in Tennessee, 1777-1945* (Knoxville: University of Tennessee Press, 1981), p. 81; Winfred E. Garrison, *The March of Faith: The Story of Religion in American Since 1865* (Westport, Conn.: Greenwood Press, 1971; Orig. pub., Harper and Brothers, 1933), pp. 76-77.

10. Winfred E. Garrison and Alfred E. DeGroot, *Disciples of Christ: A History* (St. Louis: Bethany Press, 1948), p. 359; William W. Sweet, *The Story of Religion in America* (New York: Harper and Brothers, 1930, 1939), p. 20.

11. S.A. Witmer, *The Bible College Story: Education With Dimension* (Wheaton, Ill.: The Accrediting Association of Bible Colleges, 1970), pp. 27-28.

12. Samuel S. Hill, ed., *Religion in the Southern States: A Historical Study* (Macon, Ga.: Mercer University Press, 1983), pp. 411, 277.

13. Nelson M. Blake, *A History of American Life and Thought* (New York: McGraw-Hill Book Co., 1963), p. 387; Wilma Dykeman, *Tennessee: A Bicentennial History* (New York: W.W. Norton and Co., 1975), p. 166.

14. *Christian Standard* (August 6, 1910), p. 1358.

15. Ibid. (July 21, 1883), p. 301.

16. Ibid. (August 17, 1907), p. 1377.

17. Ibid. (January 1886); quoted in Robert E. Black, *The Story of Johnson Bible College* (Kimberlin Heights, Tn.: Tennessee Valley Printing Co., 1951), p. 17.

18. *Johnson's Quarterly* (January 1890), p. 427.

19. Ibid., p. 234.

20. Ibid. (April 1891), pp. 125-126.

21. Johnson, "One Hundred Dollars," p. 4.

22. Ibid.

23. Ashley S. Johnson, *Our Life of Trust* (Knoxville: Ogden Brothers and Co., 1897), p. 5.

24. Johnson, "Story of a Check," p. 13.

25. *Christian Standard* (December 17, 1892), p. 1063.

CHAPTER TWO, Pages 43–64

1. *Knoxville Sentinel* (May 13, 1893), n.p.

2. Johnson, *Our Life of Trust*, pp. 5-6.

3. Ibid., p. 6.

4. "Ashley S. Johnson: His Witness to a Prayer-Answering God," *Johnson Bible College Newsletter* (October 1916), p. 3.

5. *Johnson Bible College Catalog* (1921-22), p. 7.

6. *17th Annual Announcements of Johnson Bible College* (1909-10), p. 6.

7. *Catalog of the School of the Evangelists* (1896), p. 11.

8. Ibid., (1893), p. 5.

9. Ibid., (1896), p. 11.

10. Ibid., (1904), back cover.

11. *Annual Announcements of the School of the Evangelists* (1906-07), p. 13.

12. *16th Annual Catalog of the School of the Evangelists* (1908-09), p. 13.

13. *17th Annual Announcements of Johnson Bible College* (1909-10), pp. 9-10.

14. *Annual Announcements of the School of the Evangelists* (1904-05), p. 6.

15. *Johnson Bible College Newsletter* (October 1916), p. 3.

16. *Christian Standard* (January 29, 1916), p. 607.

17. *Johnson Bible College Newsletter* (October 1916), p. 3.

18. *Christian Standard* (June 13, 1914), p. 1028.

19. *Catalog of the School of the Evangelists* (1896-97), pp. 6-7.

20. *Catalog of Johnson Bible College* (1919-20), p. 45.

21. *Catalog of the School of the Evangelists* (1896-97), p. 8.

22. *Johnson Bible College Newsletter* (May 1912), p. 12.

23. *Catalog of the School of the Evangelists* (1904-05), p. 4.

24. *Annual Announcements of the School of the Evangelists* (1906-07), p. 6.

25. *22nd Annual Announcements of Johnson Bible College* (1915-16), pp. 15-17.

26. *Christian Standard* (December 18, 1920), p. 1639.

27. *Johnson Bible College Catalog* (1926-27), pp. 18-19.

28. *Annual Announcements of the School of the Evangelists* (1906-07), p. 12.

29. *Catalog of the School of the Evangelists* (1904-05), p. 5.

30. The Academy was also called the Normal Department, "Night School," and, for a short time, Johnson High School.

31. *Supplement to Johnson Bible College Catalog* (1922-23), n.p.

32. *Christian Standard* (August 12, 1911), p. 1308.

33. Robert E. Black, *The Story of Johnson Bible College* (Kimberlin Heights, Tn.: Tennessee Valley Printing Co., 1951), p. 90.

34. Ibid., p. 93.

35. Ibid., pp. 92-93.

36. *Christian Standard* (June 22, 1901), p. 809.

37. Ibid. (October 11, 1902), p. 1394.

38. There are numerous accounts of the Great Fire. I have depended primarily on the newspaper article (*Knoxville Sentinel*, December 3, 1904) and Mrs. Johnson's first-hand account recorded in the 1913 Johnson Bible College student annual, Alva Ross Brown's *Standing on the Promises* (pp. 22-24), and Robert E. Black's *The Story of Johnson Bible College* (pp.76-79).

39. *Christian Standard* (December 31, 1904), p. 1890.

40. Ibid. (December 23, 1905), p. 2042.

41. *Johnson Bible College Newsletter* (1909-10), p. 4.

42. *18th Annual Announcements of Johnson Bible College* (1911-12), p. 26.

43. Ashley S. Johnson, ed., *World-wide Witness* (1907-08), p. 12.

44. *Annual Announcements of the School of the Evangelists* (1901-02), p. 14.

45. Ibid.

46. *Catalog of the School of the Evangelists* (1893), p. 4.

47. *Annual Announcements of the School of the Evangelists* (1896-97), p. 10.

48. *Blue and White* (November-December 1973), p. 1. See also *Christian Standard* (August 12, 1972).

49. Ashley S. Johnson, "Story of One Hundred Dollars," pp. 44-45.

50. *16th Annual Catalog of the School of the Evangelists* (1908-09), p. 16.

51. *Christian Standard* (December 11, 1909), p. 2178.

52. *Annual Announcements of the School of the Evangelists* (1907-08), p. 7.

53. Papers of Ashley S. Johnson, handwritten Matriculation Pledge, 1898-99.

54. *Annual Announcements of the School of the Evangelists* (1901-02), p. 9.

55. Johnson, *World-wide Witness* (October 1904), p. 1.

56. Brown, *Standing on the Promises*, pp. 33-34.

57. Ibid., p. 39.

58. *Catalog of Johnson Bible College* (1925-26), p. 7.

59. *Christian Standard* (January 24, 1925), p. 401.

60. *Catalog of Johnson Bible College* (1924-25), p. 7.

CHAPTER THREE, Pages 81-94

1. Papers of Alva Ross Brown, "Letter to Beloved Old Guard," October 22, 1927. Johnson Bible College, Kimberlin Heights, Tennessee.

2. Alva Ross Brown, *Standing on the Promises* (Knoxville: S.B. Newman and Co., 1928), p. 239.

3. *Blue and White* (March 14, 1941).

4. Papers of Alva Ross Brown. Postcards sent from Nashville, 1924. Johnson Bible College, Kimberlin Heights, Tennessee.

5. Brown, *Standing on the Promises*, p. 237.

6. Brown, "J.B.C. Faces the Issue," *Christian Standard* (July 23, 1927), p. 720.

7. "What will Happen to J.B.C. After the Death of Its Founder?" *Christian Standard* (July 27, 1912), p. 1233.

8. Papers of Ashley S. Johnson. Will of Ashley S. Johnson, October 7, 1922. Johnson Bible College, Kimberlin Heights, Tennessee.

9. Papers of Ashley S. Johnson. Last Will and Testament of Ashley S. Johnson, October 28, 1924. Johnson Bible College, Kimberlin Heights, Tennessee.

10. "J.B.C. Faces Issue," *Christian Standard* (June 23, 1927), p. 720.

11. *Christian Standard* (March 8, 1941), p. 236.

12. "What About the Future of J.B.C.?" *Christian Standard* (June 25, 1927), p. 618.

13. "J.B.C. Faces Issue," *Christian Standard* (June 23, 1927), p. 720.

14. The Johnson Junior (April 27, 1928), p. 1-2. The *Blue and White* originated in 1927 as a student paper published by the Junior Class, originally titled *The Johnson Junior*. It remained a student paper (under faculty supervision) until the late 1940s when Dr. Bell assumed its editorship. The

name was changed to *Blue and White* in October, 1928.

15. *Blue and White* (November 15, 1930), p. 1; December 24, 1931), p. 3.

16. *Blue and White* (December 24, 1931), p. 4.

17. *Christian Standard* (December 16, 1933), p. 1017.

18. The Johnson Junior (February 2, 1928), p. 1.

19. *Christian Standard* (December 21, 1935), p. 1224.

20. *Christian Standard* (January 29, 1938), p. 106.

21. See Robert E. Black's analysis in *Story of JBC*, pp. 65-67.

22. *Blue and White* (January 1, 1935), p. 3.

23. For example, see 1929-1930 *Catalog of Johnson Bible College*, p. 43.

24. *Blue and White* (March 31, 1933), p. 1.

25. Ibid. (March 29, 1930), p. 1.

26. Ibid. (March 20, 1935), p. 1.

27. Ibid. (November 30, 1929), p. 3.

28. *Christian Standard* (January 29, 1938), p. 106.

29. *Blue and White* (March 12, 1940), p. 1.

30. Reuben Ratzlaff, *Aunt Maggie: or a Life Hidden With Christ* (Kimberlin Heights, Tn.: Johnson Bible College Press, 1938).

31. *Christian Standard* (May 24, 1941), p. 547; *Blue and White* (March 14, 1941).

CHAPTER FOUR, Pages 105–122

1. Kay Watts, *The Life and Preaching of R.M. Bell* (Joplin, Mo.: College Press, 1978), pp. 115-117; Claire E. Berry, "The Life and Contribution of Robert Monroe Bell" (unpublished thesis, Division of Graduate Instruction, Butler University, 1965), p. 41.

2. Robert M. Bell, "To My Home Church," *Blue and White* (January-February 1964), p. 1.

3. Berry, "Robert Monroe Bell," p. 39.

4. Ibid., p. 48.

5. Watts, *Life and Preaching*, p. 127.

6. Berry, "Robert Monroe Bell," p. 55.

7. *Blue and White* (June 20, 1942), p. 1.

8. *Christian Standard* (April 24, 1943), p. 373.

9. *Blue and White* (October 20, 1941), p. 1.

10. *Johnson Bible College Bulletin* (1964-65), p. 23.

11. *Catalog of Johnson Bible College* (1945-46), p. 24.

12. *Blue and White* (May-June 1967), p. 1.

13. Ibid.

14. *Catalog of Johnson Bible College* (1941-42), p. 50.

15. Johnson Bible College Bulletin (1949), p. 11.

16. *Blue and White* (September 1952), p. 3.

17. Johnson Bible College Bulletin (1964-65), p. 4.

18. Black, *Story of JBC*, p. 72.

19. Ibid.

20. *Blue and White* (October-November 1952), p. 1.

21. Ibid.

22. *Christian Standard* (October 30, 1943), p. 926.

23. *Blue and White* (February 1943), p. 1.

24. Ibid. (January 1945), p. 1.

25. Ibid. (October 1944), p. 1.

26. Watts, *Life and Preaching*, p. 140.

27. *Blue and White* (Summer 1956), p. 1.

28. Ibid. (September-October 1956), p. 1.

29. "Transcript of Proceedings: J.B.C. Homecoming in Honor of Mrs. R.M. Bell," February 11, 1971, pp. 5-6.

30. *Blue and White* (January-February 1941), p. 3.

CHAPTER FIVE, Pages 143–159

1. *Blue and White* (Summer 1969), p. 1.

2. *Christian Standard* (May 20, 1979), pp. 444-445; (March 16, 1980), pp. 245-246.

3. *Blue and White* (Summer 1969), p. 4.

4. Ibid.

5. Ibid.

6. The trustees revised the purpose statement shortly after the 1991-93 catalog was printed. See *Johnson Bible College Undergraduate Catalog* (1991-1993), p. 3.

7. *Christian Standard* (November 30, 1986), pp. 1101-1102; (November 19, 1978), pp. 1072-1074.

8. Ibid., (November 30, 1986), p. 1102.

9. Ibid. (January 4, 1981), pp. 11-12.

10. *Blue and White* (Summer 1969), p. 1.

11. Ibid. (January 1980), p. 1.

12. *Christian Standard* (January 4, 1981), pp. 11-12.

13. "Johnson Bible College Faculty and Administration Guide" (1988), p. 9.

14. *Blue and White* (March 1984), p. 1.

EPILOGUE, Pages 185–191

1. *The Evangelist* (1957), p. 60.

2. *Blue and White* (May 1985), p. 2.

3. Ibid. (June 1982), pp. 1-2.

4. Ibid. (October 1989), p. 2.

5. Ibid. (April 1988), p. 1.

6. *The Evangelist* (1954), p. 17.

7. *The Apostoloi* (1943), n.p.

8. *The Crusader* (1949), n.p.

9. *Annual Announcements of the School of the Evangelists* (1907-08), p. 5.

APPENDIX A:
TRUSTEES OF JOHNSON BIBLE COLLEGE

Ashley S. Johnson (1909–1925)
Mrs. Ashley S. Johnson (1909–1927)
J. C. Johnson, Sr. (1909–?)
Charles R.L. Johnson (1909, 1925–?)
Martin Luther Pierce (1909–?)
Howard H. Groves (1909–?)
Victor P. Bowers (1909–?)
Patrick Henry Mears (1909–?)
Frederick R. Davies (1909–?)
Ritchie Ware (1909–?)
Joel Dennis Strawn (1909–?)
E. L. Barham (1925–?)
August I. Zeller (1925–1927)
Albert T. Fitts (1925–1930)
Gilbert E. Chandler (1925–1938)
W. Homer Sperry (1925–1930)
Helen Campbell Bourne (1925–1938)
S. S. Lappin (1926–1961)
Alva Ross Brown (1927–1941)
Hugh E. Steele (1927–1938)
Fred J. Riebel (1931–1938)
R. M. Bell (1938–1968)
A. Berton Clarke (1938–1972)
J. E. deGafferelly (1938–1972)
Edward L. Branham (1938–1954)
P. H. Welshimer (1938–1958)
T. K. Smith (1953–1969)
Samuel C. Taylor (1956–1964)
John Scott (1958–1969)
Wilbur Reid, Sr. (1963–1985)
Duke C. Jones (1963–1969)
James McKowen (1963–1985)
Glen Wheeler (1966–1986)
Mrs. B. D. Phillips, Sr. (1967–1983)
E. Troy Hasty (1969–present)
Fred G. Musick (1969–1984)
David L. Eubanks (1970–present)

Dennis Fulton (1970–1989)
James Cannaday (1970–1984)
Ben Hackett (1972–1987)
James Bealle (1976–present)
Lanis Kineman (1976–present)
Ralph Carnathan (1983–present)
Ralph Sproles (1984–present)
L. D. Campbell (1984–present)
Paul T. Coleman (1985–1988)
Raymond Martin (1985–1988)
Kenneth Overdorf (1986–present)
Ralph Bennett (1987–present)
Mike Mowrer (1988–present)
Roy Yeatts (1988–1992)

APPENDIX B:
ADMINISTRATORS, FACULTY, AND LIBRARIANS OF JOHNSON BIBLE COLLEGE

1893–1940

College Faculty

Ashley S. Johnson (1893–1925)
Mrs. Ashley S. Johnson (1893–1927)
Albert T. Fitts (1893–94; 1927–1940)
Adam K. Adcock (1893–?; 1912–1913)
Edwin E. Macy (1900–1902)
Miss Mary McCollough (1900–1902)
Mrs. Edwin E. Macy (1900–1902)
Miss Cordie Nichols (1900–1902)
Louis Rollings (1900–1906)
Martin Luther Pierce (1901–1912)
Nellie S. Spencer (1902–1906)
Paul Johnson Anderson (1906–1910)
St. John Halstead (1906–1909)
W. H. Trainum (1907–1908)
Edgar H. Broome (1907–1910; 1919–1921)
Howard H. Groves (1908–1921)
Hugh E Steele (1910–1915; 1931–1940)
Terry Stanley Tarr (1910–1914)
Otto Lee Dean (1910–1912)
Omar W. Hearn (1912–1913)
William H. Sperry (1912–1914; 1916–31)
Robert A. Honn (1912–1913)
Oren E. Long (1913–1917)
Charles E. Burns (1913–1919)
Curtis Wynn (1914–1917)
Walter L. Thompson (1915–1917)
Thomas H. Johnson (1917–1922; 1924–1928)
Ephraim L. Barham (1919–1925)
John F. Leggett (1920–1922)
Robert M. Bell (1921–1923; 1941–1968)
Washburn H. Elliott (1922–1928)
August I. Zeller (1924–1927)
Alva R. Brown (1924–1940)
Helen F. (Campbell) Bourne (1925–1927; 1953–1958)

Helen F. Stokes (1925–1942)
Harold Hanlin (1925–1928; 1931–1938)
Thomas B. Ford (1926–1928)
Henry R. Garrett (1926–1947)
R. D. Scott (1927–1931)
John L. McLarty (1928–1934)
William O. Lappin (1928–1959)
Mrs. W. O. Lappin (1929–1934)
J. Fred Bayless (1934–1943)
Basil F. Holt (1937–1940)
J. Alvin Keen (1937–1940)
Cecil K. Thomas (1938–1944)
Arthur A. Hyde (1940–1944)

Academy teachers, student teachers, and student librarians
John B. Dickson (1900–1902)
Clarence Purcell (1900–1902)
Mary A McCullough (1901–1902)
J. Eugene Dinger (1901–1902)
Rudolph Heike (1902–1906)
James T. Moore (1902–1903)
Edgar A. Johnston (1902–1906)
Roscoe H. Bacon (1903–1906)
Charles H. Swift (1904–1906)
Adam Reed Liverett (1904–1906)
John Grimm Engle (1904–1906)
Effie Griffitts (1906–1907)
W. H. Trainum (1907–1908)
Edgar H. Broome (1907–1910; 1919–1921)
Edward L. Branham (1907–1908)
Roy E. Weare (1908–1912)
Miss Margaret Frazier (1908–1910)
Charles W. Starr (1908–1909)
Lucius McAfee (1909–1910)
Anson S. Dowd (1909–1911)
Lehman C. Carawan (1910–1912)
Joshua L. Bell (1910–1911)
Roy Eugene Chase Simms (1910–1911)
John E. Lord (1910–1912)
Robert R. Yelderman (1911–1913)

Jonathan C. Braswell (1912–1913)
John G. Hirschler (1913–1914)
A. Roy Bemis (1913–1914)
Glen Carter (1914–1916)
Ernest W. Couch (1914–1916)
John A. Laws (1915–1918)
C. M. Anderson (1915–1916)
V. J. Murray (1915–1917)
Richard E. Brown (1916–1917)
S. M. Linkletter (1916–1917)
Gus H. Cachiaras (1916–1917)
Charles G. Rains (1917–1919)
Paul E. Chopard (1917–1919)
C. Lloyd Harris (1919–1921)
John C. Lawder (1919–1924)
Herbert A. Bourne (1921–1924)
Guy J. Wright (1921–1922)
Homer W. Haislip (1921–1922)
A. Berton Clarke (1921–1924)
Glen E. Pryor (1921–1922)
Ralph Knight (1922–1924)
H. Clay Boyts (1922–1924)
Wilfred L. Outhouse (1922–1925)
Allen J. Collins (1924–1927)
Carrol Langston (1924–1927)
Carrie Fox (1924–1925)
Oscar Sutherland (1924–1925)
Curtis Burris (1924–1927)
Gilbert Peery (1924–1927)
Francis F. Drowota, Jr. (1924–1927)
Otha L. Clary (1926–1929)
Omar L. Clary (1926–1929)
Cecil R. Hickman (1926–1929)
Mrs. O. W. Dynes (1940–1941)

1941–Current

Full–time Administrators, Faculty, and Librarians
Harry C. Wagner (1941–1946)
Dean S. Jacoby (1942–1945)

J. Spencer Holland (1942–1953)
Floyd E. Clark (1944–1979)
Paul T. Bligh (1946–1958)
John W. Lambert (1946–1949)
Delno Brown (1947–1949)
Robert E. Black (1949–1989)
Ruth Rowland (1950–1973)
Clark Rowland (1950–1973)
Fred B. Craddock (1953–1957)
Cyril C. Simkins (1956–1964)
Lee Richardson (1957–Present)
Earl B. King (1958–1963)
David L. Eubanks (1958–Present)
Lovella Richardson (1958–1985)
J. O. Pierson (1960–Present)
William R. Blevins (1963–Present)
Joel F. Rood (1965–Present)
John M. Lowe (1966–Present)
Linda R. Williams (1966–1971)
Martha James (1967–1969; 1973–1978)
Gary Weedman (1969–1976)
Janis M. Weedman (1969–1976)
Richard Robison (1969–70; 1975–1981)
Wilbur A. Reid, Jr. (1970–Present)
Michael Lacy (1971–1981)
Helen Lemmon (1971–Present)
Lillie Britton (1973–1975)
Darrell Olges (1973–1975)
Marie Garrett (1974–1977; 1980–1988)
Ben D. Lutz, Sr. (1974–Present)
Robert H. Jones (1974–1990)
Michael Dunn (1975–1978)
Philip W. Wiltshire (1975–1983)
Donald Sewell (1975–1986)
Robert Martin (1975–Present)
Stanley K. McDaniel (1976–Present)
Ronald E. Wheeler (1977–Present)
Kenneth L. Jones (1978–1986)
Gerald L. Mattingly (1978–1979, 1980–19882, 1983–1985, 1987–Present)

Chris M. Templar (1978–Present)
Richard K. Beam (1978–Present)
David A. Enyart (1979–Present)
Douglas E. Karnes (1979–Present)
Richard Phillips (1979–Present)
Norm Dungan (1981–Present)
J. Daniel Robertson (1981–Present)
Bradford C. Burnette, Jr. (1982–1990)
Linda Smith (1983–Present)
Stephen L. Smith (1983–Present)
Donald Trentham (1985–Present)
Jill Allen Lagerberg (1986–Present)
Carl B. Bridges (1987–Present)
Angela R. Robertson (1988–Present)
Dennis C. Gaertner (1989–Present)
L. Thomas Smith, Jr. (1989–Present)
W. David Reece (1990–Present)

Part–time Faculty and Librarians
Mrs. Alma Brown (1941–1943)
Stella Broome (1945–1946)
Mrs. Carl Baughman (1945–1946)
Lorraine Brown (1947–1949)
Wilson "Bill" Phifer (1949–1950)
Margaret Magill (1955–1958)
Elmer C. Lewis (1956–1958)
Pauline Williams (1963–1966)
Harold L. Noe (1968–1969; 1983–Present)
Rebecca O. Lowe (1969–Present)
Madonna Burget (1970–1971)
Martha Raile (1971; 1973–1974)
Ron Lee (1972–1973)
Wally Farnham (1972–1973)
Kenneth Overdorf (1973–1983)
Robert O. Fife (1974–75; 1980–1986)
Troy Hasty (1974–1975)
Pat Woliver (1974–1975)
Patrick Daugherty (1974–1975)
Mildred Lutz (1975–1985)
Charles Gresham (1975–1978)

David Wead (1976–1983)
Sondra Wilson (1976–1978)
Gene Davidson (1978–1979)
Joy Fisher (1979–1980)
Jennie Stillman (1980–1981)
Diane L. Darling (1981–1992)
Ralph A. Wheeler (1981–1983)
Patsy Moore (1981–1987)
Janet Gregory (1981–1982)
Jennifer Jones (1982–1985)
Billie Schneider (1983–1984)
Cynthia Murphy (1984–1985)
Steve LeMay (1985–1986)
Donna McMillan (1985–1986)
William Hoff (1986–1987; 1992–1993)
Randy Matney (1986–1988)
Rye Bell (1986–1987)
David Burnette (1986–1989)
Angela Fryer (1987–1989)
Larry Crouch (1989–1990)
Sheldon Withrow (1989–Present)
Carol Boaz (1989–Present)
Sam Darden (1989–Present)
Susan Dunlap (1990–Present)
Brian Lakin (1990–1992)
William Justice (1991–1992)
Deborah Berkley (1991–Present)
Jennifer Watt (1992–Present)
Robert Lozano (1992–Present)

Information for the early years of the College may be incomplete. The author and the College would welcome additions or corrections.

APPENDIX C:
ALUMNI DISTINGUISHED SERVICE
AWARD RECIPIENTS

1966 H. Ancil Bourne
       A. Berton Clarke
1967 Gertrude W. Kostik
       Mrs. R.M. Bell
1968 Duke C. Jones
1969 Edith H. Snow
       Robert E. Black
1970 Floyd E. Clark
1971 Mildred W. Phillips
1972 D. Lee Richardson
1973 W. Clark Rowland
1974 John U. Phelps
1975 Lloyd D. Sanders
       Frank and Pauline Williams
1976 Russell and Jean Morgan
       Helen Stokes Kerns
1977 S. Edward Tesh
1978 Harold F. Hanlin
       Alan Buzard
1980 Earl B. and Marie King, Sr.
1981 Charles Sublett
       Konstantin Jaroshevich
1982 Wilbur A. Reid, Sr.
       Claude Swaggerty
       William Sylvester and Ruth Hughes
       George A. Rickard, Sr.
1983 Brad Burnette
       Levy Hodges
       Ellen Beal Thomas
1984 William and Virginia Loft
       Donald and Mary Gally
       Madonna Burget
1985 Harry L. Hamilton
       Clinton and Phyllis Thomas
       Lee Earl Acuff
       John Hill

1986 Ben and Pat Merold
       Fred Millard
1987 Dennis Fulton
       Robert H. Jones, Jr.
1988 Marvin Matthews
       Mayo and Janet Proctor
1989 Ali Jarman
       Harland Cary
1990 Ralph Lee Johnson
       J.B. and Gladys Smith
1991 Dean and Judy Davis
       Harry and Janet Holloway
       C.Y. and Pat Kim
       Samuel L. Fleming
1992 Lanis and Kathryn Kineman
       Cyril and Mary Simkins

APPENDIX D:
HONORARY DEGREES AWARDED
BY JOHNSON BIBLE COLLEGE

	Ashley S. Johnson	Master of Arts
	Albert T. Fitts	Master of Arts
1934	Edwin Errett	Doctor of Laws
1934	Walter M. White	Doctor of Laws
1936	Henry R. Garrett	Doctor of Literature
1950	Thornton Miller	Doctor of Laws
1957	Joseph Dampier	Doctor of Laws
1959	William Otis Lappin	Doctor of Laws
1960	Oren E. Long	Doctor of Laws
1966	Robert M. Bell	Doctor of Divinity
1968	Floyd E. Clark	Doctor of Divinity
1969	A. Berton Clarke	Doctor of Divinity
1969	Mildred Welshimer Phillips	Doctor of Fine Arts
1969	Wilbur Reid, Sr.	Doctor of Divinity
1971	Robert E. Black	Doctor of Divinity
1974	G. H. Cachiaras	Doctor of Divinity
1976	F. Berton Doyle	Doctor of Divinity
1978	Glen Wheeler	Doctor of Divinity

1980   Myron J. Taylor   Doctor of Divinity

1984   David L. Eubanks   Doctor of Divinity

Information concerning honorary degrees is incomplete. The author and the College would welcome additions or corrections.

SELECTED BIBLIOGRAPHY

Bell, Robert Monroe. *Reasoning Together.* Joplin, Mo.: College Press, 1969.

Berry, Claire E. "The Life and Contribution of Robert Monroe Bell." M.A. thesis, Division of Graduate Instruction, Butler University, 1965.

Black, Robert E. *The Story of Johnson Bible College.* Kimberlin Heights, Tenn.: Tennessee Valley Printing Co., 1951.

Brown, Alva Ross. *Our Lord's Most Sublime Words.* Kingsport: Southern Publishers, 1930.

_____. *Standing on the Promises.* Knoxville: S.B. Newman and Co., 1928.

_____. *Faith, Prayer, Work: Being the Story of Johnson Bible College with Choice Quotations from Ashley S. Johnson.* n.p., n.d.

Campbell, Jeffrey. "A Comparative Study of Curriculum Development of Johnson Bible College and Moody Bible Institute." M.A.R.E. thesis, Emmanuel School of Religion, 1970.

Dutka, Denis. "The Doctrines of Ashley Sidney Johnson as Found in His Writings." M.A.B.R. thesis, Harding College Graduate School of Religion, 1966.

Eagen, L. John. *The Bible College in American Higher Education.* American Association of Bible Colleges, 1981.

Eubanks, David L. "An Historical Account of the Development of Johnson Bible College." M.Th. thesis, Johnson Bible College, 1958.

_____. *Jesus, the Last Word.* Cincinnati: Standard Publishing, 1973.

Johnson, Ashley S. *Bible Readings and Sermon Outlines on the Christian Plea*. Knoxville: Ogden Brothers & Co., 1900.

_____. *Correspondence Bible College*. Knoxville: Ogden Brothers and Co., 1901.

_____. *Condensed Biblical Cyclopedia*. Louisville: Guide Printing and Publishing Co., 1896.

_____. *Evangelistic and Expository Sermons*. Knoxville: S.B. Newman and Co., 1896.

_____. *The Great Controversy*.

_____. *The Holy Spirit and the Human Mind*. Knoxville: Gaut-Ogden Company, 1903.

_____. *Johnson's Sermons on the Two Covenants*. Knoxville: Ogden Brothers, 1899.

_____. *Johnson's Speeches*. Knoxville: Ogden Brothers, 1895.

_____. *Letters to a Young Methodist Preacher*. Knoxville: Ogden Brothers and Co., 1897.

_____. *Opening the Book of the Seven Seals*. Knoxville: Ogden Brothers and Co., 1896.

_____. *Our Life of Trust*. Knoxville: Ogden Brothers and Co., 1897.

_____. *Out of Darkness Into Light*. Louisville: Guide Printing and Publishing Co., 1894.

_____. *The Resurrection and the Future Life*. Knoxville: Knoxville Lithographing Co., 1913.

_____. *The Story of a Check for $100*. Knoxville: Ogden Brothers and Co., 1900.

_____. *Ten Lessons in How to Read, Understand, and Remember the Bible.* Louisville: Guide Printing and Publishing Co., 1896.

_____. *The Tennessee Evangelist.* Cincinnati: Standard Publishing Co., 1886.

_____. *The Self-Interpreting New Testament.* Knoxville: Ogden Brothers and Company, 1898.

Reid, Wilbur A., Jr. "A Bibliographic Handbook of the Life and Unpublished Work of Robert Monroe Bell." M.R.E. thesis, Emmanuel School of Religion, 1973.

Smith, L. Thomas, Jr. "Context and Response: An Interpretive History of the School of the Evangelists (Johnson Bible College) 1893-1909." M.A.R. thesis, Emmanuel School of Religion, 1986.

Ware, C.C. *South Carolina Disciples of Christ: A History.* Charleston: Christian Churches of South Carolina, 1967.

Watts, Kathryn. *The Life and Preaching of R.M. Bell.* Joplin, Mo.: College Press, 1978.

Witmer, S.A. *The Bible College Story: Education with Dimension.* Wheaton, Ill.: The Accrediting Association of Bible Colleges, 1970.

INDEX